The Royal National Eisteddfod of Wales

Iolo Morganwg.

The Royal National Eisteddfod of Wales

Dillwyn Miles
The Herald Bard

Christopher Davies
Swansea

Copyright © Dillwyn Miles 1978

First published by
Christopher Davies (Publishers) Ltd.
52 Mansel Street
Swansea SA1 5EL

Set in 10/12 Baskerville

*Printed in Wales by
Salesbury Press Ltd.
Swansea*

ISBN 0 7154 0323 0

In memory of Joyce

CONTENTS

ILLUSTRATIONS

PREFACE

One would have expected that so historic and colourful an institution as the Royal National Eisteddfod of Wales would have books and books written about it. In truth, with the exception of a bilingual handbook written for distribution to schools, there is no published work that is easily available to the general reader.

It was Sir Alun Talfan Davies, Q.C., who suggested to me that I should write something to meet this shortcoming, and I undertook the project in the innocent belief that it would not be too arduous. In the event, it proved to be a formidable task, and one's highest hope is that this book will inspire others to pursue more detailed studies of a fascinating and seemingly inexhaustible subject. The complete story can never be told, sad to say, for much of it was never recorded; much lies concealed in letters and private papers, and much was planned by word of mouth and executed spontaneously without being committed to writing, and documents have disappeared without trace, or to reappear mysteriously in the United States of America. And there are the incidental *minutiae* that one gathers only by long communion with veterans and *cognoscenti*.

From its early beginnings as a confined contest among the bards, the Eisteddfod has developed into a unique public festival at which tens of thousands of people gather each year. It is a Welsh festival, so much so that no one has invented any other name for it in any other language. In every language in the world it is known as the Eisteddfod.

Its affairs are conducted, naturally, in the Welsh language, but facilities are available for those who do not speak or understand Welsh. As the last great stronghold of the language it is essential that it should be uncompromising in the matter of the 'all-Welsh rule'.

The contribution of the National Eisteddfod to literature, music and the arts is beyond question. From this nomadic metropolis have also emerged ideas which have led to the establishment of our national institutions — the University of Wales, the National Library of Wales, the National Museum of Wales and the Llangollen International Musical Eisteddfod.

A hundred years ago *The London Review* informed its readers that 'the Eisteddfod is now a yearly joke which the world thinks none the worse for its being perpetuated at the expense of a race which is gradually becoming extinct', and there has been no shortage of criticism and censure ever since, even by its most fervent friends. It has grown too large, they say; there is too much extraneous activity, too much party politics, too much religion, too much boozing (off the field, of course). The views of many were succinctly expressed by the Rev. Trebor Lloyd Evans: 'The Eisteddfod should be an Eisteddfod, not a Parliament for Wales nor a Festival nor a Cymanfa nor a Sasiwn nor a jamboree.'

'The Eisteddfod', wrote Mr. Dafydd Morris Jones, Secretary of the Aberystwyth Eisteddfod in 1952, 'is an amalgam made up of a competitive meeting, a national pageant and a great reunion.' Above all, a great reunion — 'casglu'r Cymry 'nghyd', the ingathering of the Welsh from the four corners of the earth.

I am grateful to the former Archdruid Brinli and to Mr Ernest Roberts, formerly Secretary to the Eisteddfod Council, for reading the manuscript of this book; to the former Archdruid and Recorder Gwyndaf for permission to reproduce the line drawings of Gorsedd regalia; to Mr John Rees, Carmarthen, for providing the historical photographs from the collection of his late father, the Grand Sword Bearer Gwallter Dyfi, and to many others who, knowingly or otherwise, gave me some useful information.

Haverfordwest, 1978   DILLWYN MILES

THE EISTEDDFOD

No one knows when the first eisteddfod was held, or where it took place. No early chronicler wrote: 'In this year the Welsh held their first Eisteddfod'. In no proud village is there a stone pillar inscribed: 'On this spot was held the earliest Eisteddfod of all'. The beginnings are lost in the half-light of time, when priest and prophet and poet are not easy to tell apart.

The tradition of verse-making in Wales goes back to pre-Christian times. The druids, who had responsibility for the education of the young and for the intellectual life of all, taught entirely by means of poetry orally transmitted. Caesar, in his *Gallic Wars*, states that 'young Britons sat at the feet of druids to learn verses', and that they learned a great number of verses, some remaining twenty years in this discipline. They would not commit their teaching to writing and had no books. It was through the medium of verse, easier to commit to memory, that they transferred their ideas of the nature of things and of the immortality of the soul.

The Celts believed that the power of speech was greater than physical strength; they re-christened Hercules 'Ogmios' and made him a god of eloquence. The absence of books caused additional emphasis to be placed on speech, which led to oratorial vigour and a concentration on expression by word of mouth rather than by writing.

The Romans feared the influence and the power of the druids to such an extent that they dispatched the distinguished general Suetonius Paulinus to attack the centre of druidic power, which was Anglesey. Tacitus states that the people there were warlike and that the island was a haven for others of like spirit. He goes on to say that this warlike spirit got its moral boost from the druids, who were present on the island in considerable numbers, and so Suetonius came in 61 A.D. and annihilated them. Thus perished a people described by Nora Chadwick, in her book *The Druids*, as 'the most enlightened and civilising spiritual influence in pre-historic Europe'.

The druids were philosophers and priests who made use of poetry as a teaching device. Posidonius, writing in about 100 B.C., states that poets in Britain were called *bardoi*, which is the Celtic form of the Welsh *bardd* (bard) and that chieftains of pre-Roman Britain had bards in their retinues or at their courts.

The earliest Welsh bards of whom there is record were poets at the courts of princes in north Britain in the sixth century. Taliesin was *pencerdd* (chief poet) at the court of Urien, prince of Rheged, the land around Merin Rheged (Solway Firth) with its capital at Caer Lliwelydd (Carlisle). He wrote poems in praise of his prince, bold hero in battle and generous host at his hearth. He sang of the bravery of Urien and of his son, Owain, plundering the Angles of Bernicia and leaving their dead 'with the light on their eyes' on the battlefield. He laments the death of Owain, who punished the enemy 'as a wolf would pursue sheep', and he immortalised father and son so that they became legendary heroes. He also praised the hospitality he had received at other courts, in Wales as well as in northern Britain, indicating the close contact that existed between these Celtic areas, separated by the invading Saxons.

Aneirin was chief poet at the court of Mynyddog Mwynfawr, prince of Manaw Gododdin, the land to the south of Aber Gweryd (the Firth of Forth), with its capital at Caeredin (Edinburgh). Mynyddog had gathered together at his court three hundred young noblemen whom he trained and feasted for a whole year in preparation for battle against the Angles of Deira and Bernicia at Catraeth (Catterick). They fought for a week, against overwhelming numbers, until they were all killed, save the poet Aneirin. Like Taliesin, he wrote of contemporary heroes whom he knew personally during their training at Caeredin. He praised them one by one and extolled the virtues of each: he is sorrowful and yet proud of the men who went to Catraeth:

> Gwŷr a aeth Gatraeth oedd ffraeth eu llu;
> Glasfedd eu hancwyn, a gwenwyn fu.
> Trichant trwy beiriant yn catäu,
> A gwedi elwch tawelwch fu.

(The men who went to Catraeth were a willing band. New mead their joy, but poison it became. Three hundred by order went to battle. After the merriment, silence.)

The poet always held an exalted position among the Welsh and it would appear that his highest achievement was to become a *pencerdd* (chief poet) at the court of a king or a prince. The *pencerdd* ranked high among the twenty-four officers of the court and sat next to the *edling*, or heir apparent, in the hall, and had the right to sit next to the king. This was a greatly coveted position and one for which there was considerable rivalry, which implies that some form of test or contest had to be undergone before the *pencerdd's* chair could be achieved. It may be that in this contest is to be found the embryo of the *eisteddfod:* the chair of the Chaired Bard at this year's National Eisteddfod is undoubtedly a survival of the chair occupied by the *pencerdd* at the courts of the princes.

Dr Thomas Parry, in his *Hanes Llenyddiaeth Cymru* (History of Welsh Literature), points out that the poet obtained his living by his craft, as did the cobbler or the carpenter, and that it was therefore essential that he should excel in it. His only way of doing so was by becoming a disciple of an older or superior poet, who taught not only the arts of poetry but also the use of words, history, legends and heraldry. In order to protect their craft, the poets formed an order, like a guild of craftsmen, to which entry was not easy. Little is known of this early guild prior to the *Law* of Hywel Dda, which lists the three orders of bards: *pencerdd* (chief poet), *bardd teulu* (family poet) and *cerddor* (minstrel).

A *pencerdd* is described in the *Law* as 'a bard who has won a chair' and, as one of the traditional officers of court, he exercised authority over other poets and always sang first in hall. His harp was valued at one hundred and twenty pence, and his tuning horn at twenty pence. The *bardd teulu* was also one of the officers of the court, but of a lower status. He received land and a horse and a harp from the king, and a gold ring from the queen, to whom it was his duty to sing whenever requested. The *cerddor* had no defined rights, but he is mentioned as a member of the royal retinue.

These legal rights ceased to exist with the loss of Welsh independence in 1282, but the spirit of the law continued for several centuries. After the passing of the kings and princes, the poet had to rely on the patronage and hospitality he obtained in the houses of the nobility. He no longer held the security of a court official and his status was greatly diminished. The *pencerdd* lost his authority and his precedence among poets faded, but the poets themselves made efforts to maintain the old order by gathering together at irregular intervals at meetings which laid the foundation for the Eisteddfod as it stands today.

The Meaning of 'Eisteddfod'

The word *eisteddfod* has a wide range of meanings. In the fourteenth century the poet Iolo Goch referred to the episcopal seat or throne of St. David at Menevia as *Yr eisteddfod ym maenol Dewi Mynyw*, and it was used to signify a residence, abode, assembly, synod, session, council, conference or congress, but from the fifteenth century onward it acquired a specialized meaning and was thereafter customarily used to describe a gathering of bards and musicians. Even so, its meaning has changed with the centuries. It referred to the fifteenth century assembly of poets, where the rules of Welsh poetry were reviewed, and to the sixteenth century meetings where bards were examined and the more worthy approved. It also described the small groups of poets who met in taverns all over Wales in the eighteenth century to weave verses and to hail the champion among them as 'chaired bard'. It was used for the village competitive meetings where the first prize was half a crown placed in a satin bag lovingly embroidered and equipped with a ribbon to hang around the proud winner's neck, and it is used for the great national annual festival which now costs a fortune to stage.

Early Beliefs

Nineteenth century historians claimed that *eisteddfodau* had been held regularly from the fifth century, and believed that 'the records take us back to the time of Prydain ab Aedd Mawr, who is said to have lived about a thousand years before the Christian era, and who established the Gorsedd as an institution to perpetuate the works of the poets and musicians'. Owain, son of Magnus Maximus, it was written, first brought order and discipline to the eisteddfod in about 375 A.D. Maelgwn of Llandaf, an uncle of St. Teilo, was reputed to have arranged a festival at Caerleon. Taliesin was believed to have held a competition for the chair at Caer Gwyrosydd in the year 517. Maelgwn, prince of Gwynedd, patron of an eisteddfod held at Conway in 540, mischievously commanded all competitors to swim the river before competing, which caused the harps of the musicains to warp and gave the poets a clear field. At an eisteddfod reputed to have been held in the ninth century under Geraint y Bardd Glas, it is said that *cynghanedd*[1] was established as a constituent of verse. But there appear to be no reports of any eisteddfod held between that date and 1070, when

---

[1] Cynghanedd is explained on page 149.

Rhys ap Tewdwr, prince of South Wales, was reputed to have returned from a long exile in Brittany with new rules of poetry which he imparted to the bards at an eisteddfod held at Carmarthen, or was it Neath? It is also claimed that in the eleventh century the eisteddfod of Tir Iarll, in Glamorgan was established. The patrons were the Earls of Gloucester, who had endowed the eisteddfod with arable lands at Llangynwyd and a chair to be kept in the church there. Later in that century, there are rumours of bardic feasts to which bards and musicians were invited 'as they had been by King Arthur'. Cadwgan ap Bleddyn was said to have held such a feast at Cardigan Castle in 1107, and Gruffydd ap Rhys invited 'all who came in peace from Gwynedd and Powys and Deheubarth and Morgannwg and the Marches and prepared for them all the delicacies in food and drink, and contests in wisdom and entertainment with singing and musical instruments... and masks and mysteries and manly games' at a similar feast at Ystrad Tywi.

Edward Jones (Bardd y Brenin), writing in about 1800, stated that 'the eisteddfod was a triennial assembly of the Bards (held usually at Aberffraw, the royal seat of the Prince of North Wales formerly, situated in Anglesey; likewise Dynevawr, the royal castle of the Prince of South Wales, in Carmarthenshire; and Mathravael, the royal palace of the Princes of Powys, in Montgomeryshire) for the regulation of Poetry and Music, for the purpose of conferring degrees, and of advancing to the Chair of the Eisteddfod, by the decision of a Poetical and Musical contest, some of the rival candidates; or establishing in that honourable seat the *Chief Bard*, who already occupied it.'

He illustrates the peculiar views held concerning the origin of the eisteddfod and Llew Tegid, a century later, explains that 'the enthusiasts on one side maintain that the rites and ceremonies now attached to the National Festival have come down unimpaired and unaltered from the unknown ages of the pre-Christian era, and that their sacredness is second only to that of Holy Writ. The extreme advocates on the other side assert with great confidence that much of the ritual attached to the Gorsedd, at the present day, is the invention of the Bards of the fifteenth and fourteenth centuries. Both these zealots form, probably, a small minority, a very small minority of the inhabitants of Wales, who attend the annual festival, in thousands, year after year. The great majority live in a hazy world of uncertainty and view these proceedings in a sort of semi-sacred indifference. If ever they are brought to the prosaic and un-eisteddfodic process of fixing dates to past events, they mark the origin of their National pride, *ers miloedd o flynyddoedd, cyn cof, cyn cred*, and other vague conjectures, which need no further translation than "in the days of long ago".'

Only recently has it been possible to cull the authentic facts from an accumulation of fiction produced by romantic historians and eccentrics.

Bardic Rivalry

Although there are no proven records of early eisteddfodau, there are references which indicate that the bards gathered together in competitive session and, more particularly, for the purpose of formulating and enforcing the rules of their craft in order to keep out impostors and the incompetent.

In the *Law* of Hywel Dda it was laid down that the Court Judge was entitled to receive gifts from whoever was victorious when there was a competition for a chair, which suggests that there was a regulated contest for the chair in the tenth century. The *Law* confirmed the established position of the court poet: 'sef fydd Pencerdd bardd wedi yr enillo cadair' (a chief poet shall be a poet who has already won a chair).

Evidence of the rivalry for the office of *pencerdd* is found in the bardic disputation that took place between Cynddelw Brydydd Mawr and Seisyll Bryffwrch in 1132 for the post of chief poet at the court of the new king of Powys, Madog ap Maredudd. Seisyll claimed descent from a long line of poets and scoffed at Cynddelw for the lack of poetic tradition in his family. He sang the praises of the Lord Rhys, prince of Deheubarth, and composed elegiac odes on the death of Owain Gwynedd, king of Gwynedd, in 1170, and of his son Iorwerth who, by his wife Marared, daughter of Madog ap Maredudd, was the father of Llywelyn the Great. Cynddelw, who was chosen *pencerdd*, described himself as a master teacher who taught the most promising poets, exercising the strictest discipline of the poet's craft. He sang the praises of the princes of Powys, Gwynedd and Deheubarth, and in so doing so he may have been the first poet to have ranged over the whole of Wales. He is regarded as the leading *pencerdd* of the twelfth century and much of his work has survived, including his love poem to Eve, the daughter of Madog ap Maredudd. As a tried warrior of noble birth he was able to declare his love of his patron's daughter and to send to her, as his *llatai* (love-messenger), a 'proud and lively stallion',

> Cyfleuer gwawr dydd pan ddwyre hynt
> Cyfliw eira gorwyn gorwydd Epynt

(As bright as the dawn when day begins, of the colour of the whitest snow on the wooded slopes of Epynt).

Many of the court poets of the twelfth and thirteenth centuries are known to us by name; Meilyr and his son Gwalchmai and his grandsons, Einion and Meilyr, Gwynfardd Brycheiniog, Philip Brydydd, Y Prydydd Bychan, Dafydd Benfras and Gruffudd ab yr Ynad Coch. Many of these poets were of noble origin and some of them fought in battle and wrote love poems to ladies of high rank. Their number included two poet-princes, Hywel ab Owain Gwynedd and Owain Cyfeiliog, prince of Powys. Hywel was a lyric poet who sang of the beauty of his native Gwynedd and of its maidens:

> Caraf ei morfa a'i mynyddedd,
> A'i chaer ger ei choed a'i chain diredd,
> A'i dolydd a'i dwfr a'i dyffrynnedd,
> A'i gwylain gwynion a'i gwymp wragedd.

(I love her marsh and her mountains, her fort by her woods and her fair acres, her meadows, her rivers, her valleys, and her white sea-gulls and her beautiful women).

Owain Cyfeiliog is remembered by his dramatic poem *Hirlas Owain*. Following a night expedition to free a prisoner, Owain feasts his warriors in his taper-lit hall and calls the bearer of the *hirlas*, the long blue horn mounted with silver and gold that held the mead, to attend liberally to the needs of the warriors. He names each in turn with words of praise, and when the *hirlas* comes to an empty place:

> Ochan Grist! mor wyf drist o'r anaelau
> O goll Moreiddig, mawr ei eisiau

(In the name of Christ, I groan with pain at the loss of Moreiddig; much will he be missed). The theme is redolent of Aneirin's *Gododdin* and the content reveals that Owain was familiar with the works of poets of the sixth century.

The death of Llywelyn ap Gruffydd in 1282 brought the system of princely patronage to a close. Gruffudd ab yr Ynad Coch, in his brilliant elegy to the last Prince, felt that the end of the world had come, certainly of the world of the Welsh poets: disaster had befallen the land and hearts were frozen with fear:

> Poni welwch chwi hynt y gwynt a'r glaw?
> Poni welwch chwi'r deri'n ymdaraw? . . .
> Pa beth y'n gedir i ohiriaw?

(Do you not see the way of the wind, and the rain? Do you not see the oaks battle?... Why are we left to linger?).

After a period of dark oppression a new class of nobility arose to provide patronage for the bards. They could not afford to maintain the style of the princes, and so the bards had to depend on more than one patron and wander from one house to another in search of hospitality. Thus began *cylch clera*, an organised system for visiting the houses of the nobility by wandering bards and minstrels once in every three years. The high seasons for such visits were Easter, Whitsun and Christmastide.

These itinerant minstrels correspond to the continental *clerici vagantes*, or the *Goliardi* of the Middle Ages. They were known as *y glêr*, a word borrowed from the Irish *cleir* (wandering bards and musicians) and, more disparagingly, as *clêr y bôn* (the lowest grade of poetaster) or *clêr y dom* (poetasters of the dung). In the *Law* of Hywel Dda they are dubbed *croesaniaid* (lewd, ribald rhymers). Contemporary accounts indicate that they were generally regarded as parasites and that efforts to control their numbers were being made.

Philip Brydydd, who referred to himself as 'chaired poet' in the court of Prince Rhys Gryg, the rebellious son of the Lord Rhys, and claimed to be in the same noble tradition as the leading court poets traceable to Taliesin, states that the guardians of that tradition had been driven to take action against *gofeirdd, geufeirdd* and *gwagfeirdd* (poetasters, false poets and vain bards) throughout South Wales.

Gruffudd ap Cynan

From the twelfth century onward efforts were made to discipline the bards by formulating regulations to improve standards, and rules to govern their behaviour. There is a persistent tradition that an attempt in this direction was made by Gruffudd ap Cynan (1054-1137).

Gruffudd was the son of Cynan ap Iago, a prince of Gwynedd who had found refuge among the Danes of Dublin following the murder of his father, Iago ab Idwal, king of Gwynedd, by his own men in 1039. He married Ragnhildr, grand-daughter of Sitric of the Silken Beard, and thus allied himself with the royal Scandinavian house of Dublin. Gruffudd endeavoured to regain his patrimony with the aid of the Norsemen and landed at Abermenai in 1073, but he had to return to Ireland. In 1081 he landed at Porth Clais, the harbour of the monks of St. David's, where he was joined by Rhys ap Tewdwr who had recently been dislodged as king of Deheubarth. Together they set off from the cathedral city with the blessing of the bishop and, after a day's march, defeated the usurpers at the battle of Mynydd Carn, an unidentified site. It was an important battle, in that it established the two great dynasties of Gwynedd and Deheubarth. It also marked the birth of a Welsh literary revival which followed the resuscitation of national spirit under the leadership of Gruffudd ap Cynan.

Gruffudd is believed to have brought with him from Ireland a number of bards and musicians for his court in Gwynedd who were instrumental in reforming the rules of poetry and music in Wales, and it was held that Gruffudd had given his approval to these reforms under a 'Statute', not only to improve standards but also to bring order among itinerant minstrels. There is a tradition that an eisteddfod was held in Caerwys in Flintshire 'before the prince Gruffudd ap Cynan in person' for the purpose of eliminating 'the vain weeds' that had grown amongst poets and musicians. There are no means of confirming or denying these traditions but it is significant that they were accepted as fact and used to give authority to the arrangements for eisteddfodau held in the sixteenth century. Gruffudd, as a patron of the arts, had his own *telynor pencerdd* (chief harpist), Cellan, who was killed in battle in 1094, and the *pencerdd* at his royal court at Aberffraw was Meilyr Brydydd.

Meilyr was the earliest of the *Gogynfeirdd*, the poets of the twelfth and thirteenth century, and the first of a line of hereditary bards on the Irish pattern holding land in return for their eulogies to their patrons. He wrote a poem 'prophesying' the fate of the battle of Mynydd Carn and an elegy on the death of Gruffudd in 1137 in which he praised his patron for his generosity:

Cyn myned mab Cynan i dan dywawd
Cefid yn ei gyntedd medd a bragawd

(Before the son of Cynan was laid under the sand, there was mead and honeyed ale to be had in his hall).

His son, Gwalchmai ap Meilyr, in a poem to his patron Owain Gwynedd, son and heir to Gruffudd ap Cynan wrote: 'My father sang the praises of his royal father.'

Cardigan Castle, 1176

Rhys ap Tewdwr was killed, resisting the Norman advance near Brecon, in 1093. His death opened the flood gates which led to the

Norman occupation of south and west Wales, including the kingdom of Deheubarth. His infant son, Gruffydd, was taken to Ireland where he was reared until he returned to Wales in 1118. He eventually reached an accommodation with King Henry I and settled in Caeo in Carmarthenshire. There, in 1132, by his wife Gwenllian, daughter of Gruffudd ap Cynan, was born his younger son Rhys who was to assume the mantle of the old kings of Deheubarth. When Rhys was four years old his mother, in her husband's absence, led an attack against Kidwelly Castle, the stronghold of Maurice de Londres, and was killed fighting outside the town on a field that has ever since been known as Maes Gwenllian. Rhys himself was on the field of battle at the age of thirteen and, by 1155, he had obtained dominion over Deheubarth. He entered into a compact with Henry II in 1171 whereby he yielded the title of king of Deheubarth and became justiciar of South Wales and was known henceforth as 'The Lord Rhys'.

The Lord Rhys bestowed his patronage on religion and on the arts. Bards and Musicians enjoyed visiting his court at Dinefwr and received handsome rewards for doing so. Seisyll Bryffwrch recounted his bravery in several battles, Cynddelw Brydydd Mawr praised his generosity and spoke of his love of poetry, and Gwynfardd Brycheiniog sang his praise in his *Awdyl yr Arglwydd Rhys* (Ode to the Lord Rhys) some time after 1172.

The Lord Rhys moved his court in 1171 from Dinefwr to Cardigan and it was there that he held an event which was described in *Brut y Tywysogion* (the Chronicles of the Princes), under the year 1176, as *gwledd arbennig* (a special feast): 'The Lord Rhys held a special feast in Cardigan castle and arranged two manners of contest, the one between the poets and bards, and the other between harpists, *crwth* players, pipers and other musicians, and he gave two chairs for the winners, whom he enriched with the most generous gifts. A young man from his own court was victorious in the musical contest and men from Gwynedd excelled in poetry. All the other competitors received from The Lord Rhys all that they asked for, so that no one was disappointed. And that feast was proclaimed a year before it took place throughout Wales and England and Scotland and Ireland and many other countries'. To it, we are told, 'there repaired all the musicians of Wales and some also from England and Scotland', and among the competing poets, it seems, were the gifted poet-princes, Owain Cyfeiliog of Powys and Hywel ab Owain Gwynedd. By all accounts the occasion was a most enjoyable one, with much feasting and merrymaking!

This *gwledd arbennig*, proclaimed a year in advance with its offering of prizes for poetry and music and its ingathering of poets and musicians, bears considerable resemblance to the eisteddfod of today, and it may well be described as the earliest eisteddfod for which we have a written record.

No such records are available for the three 'Renaissance Eisteddfodau' which were claimed to have been held between 1328 and 1330, the first at Gwern-y-clepa in Bassaleg under the patronage of Ifor Hael (Ivor the Generous). This was the name given to his patron, Ifor ap Llywelyn, lord of Bassaleg, by Dafydd ap Gwilym, who is said to have won the chair at the Gwern-y-clepa eisteddfod. The second is reputed to have been held at Dol-goch in Meirioneth and the third, in 1330, at Marchwiail in Maelor under the patronage of Roger de Mortimer, the first Earl of March. It is also claimed than an eisteddfod was held at Penrhys in Glamorgan under the patronage of Owain Glyndŵr.

The Bardic 'Grammar'

Even though there are no authentic accounts of early eisteddfodau or of other procedures for regulating the bardic orders, there is evidence of a sustained effort to provide means of educating the bards. This was now done through the written word, the earliest example of which is found in a bardic 'Grammar', *Cerddwriaeth Cerd Dafawd*, compiled by Einion Offeiriad (Einion the priest) during the early part of the fourteenth century. Einion is said to have dedicated the Grammar to Sir Rhys ap Gruffydd, the most influential Welshman of his time who held extensive properties in West Wales and who died at Carmarthen in 1356, and to whom he also sang an *awdl*. The name of Dafydd Ddu Athro from Hiraddug in Flintshire is associated with the Grammar, and it is considered that he added to Einion's original work.

The Grammar was a treatise on bardic instruction, and it also contained an abbreviated version of the Latin grammar used in schools during the Middle Ages which enabled the rustic poet to gain some knowledge that was otherwise available only at schools and colleges. It gathered together the ancient and complicated metrical devices, some as old as the *Gododdin*, and arranged them in twenty-four metrical forms or measures which, after revisions in the following century, have remained unchanged until the present day.[1]

---

[1] See *The Twenty-four Measures*, p. 155.

Carmarthen, *c*. 1451

The profusion of itinerant bards continued to cause embarrassment to their patrons and, in 1402, during the reign of King Henry IV, Parliament enacted a law to get rid of 'many diseases and mischiefs which have happened before this time in the land of Wales by many wasters, rhymers, minstrels and other vagabonds', so that they would not be a burden on the country. Welsh poets were thus classified with vagabonds and beggars and liable to be put in the stocks or thrown into jail. Reputable poets had to find ways and means of protecting themselves against such punishment and this was achieved through a system of graduation and by the granting of licences to go on bardic circuits. Licences were occasionally granted at wedding feasts: Tudur Aled had his first degree as a bard conferred on him at a marriage feast at the hall of Ieuan ab Ithel Fychan of Tegeingl. The licence granted to Gruffudd Hiraethog, bard and herald, to go on circuit was signed by James Vaughan, Hugh Lewis and Lewys Morgannwg in 1546, and is still in existence. But the rules and regulations governing the craft of poetry were formulated at eisteddfodau, such as the eisteddfod held at Carmarthen *c*. 1451, and the first to be described by that name.

The Carmarthen eisteddfod was not so much a competitive event as an occasion for tightening the control over the bardic orders. It was held under the patronage of Gruffudd ap Nicolas of Dinefwr, the most powerful figure in West Wales in the middle of the fifteenth century. One report states that the event was spread over three months at Gruffudd's castle at Dinefwr; others maintain that it lasted two or three weeks and that it took place at the New Town, Dinefwr.

The main prizes were carried off by men from Tegeingl. The prize for the best harpist, a silver harp, was awarded to Cynwrig Bencerdd of Holywell, and a silver tongue was awarded to Rhys Bwtting of Prestatyn, the best singer to the accompaniment of the harp.

Gruffudd ap Nicolas judged the poets and awarded the silver chair to Dafydd ab Edmwnd, a gentleman-poet from Hanmer in Flintshire. Ieuan Llawdden, a native of Loughor, and other poets from South Wales, accused Dafydd of having bribed Gruffudd ap Nicolas, but ab Edmwnd's competence was beyond question. He was not only a master craftsman but also a poet of considerable vision and imagination who sang mostly of love and beauty and, in particular of the loveliness of women. The nun he compared to a summer moon, with the concealing night her habit:

I leuad haf ail wyd di,
A nos gudd yn wisg iddi.

Of him it has been written that 'he touched a word as though it were the leaf of a rose or the string of a harp.'

The chair was awarded to Dafydd ab Edmwnd not so much for the beauty of his poetry as for his revision and modification of the twenty-four metres, which had been established during the previous century by Einion Offeiriad and Dafydd Ddu Athro from traditional forms that had been evolved from the sixth century onward. He introduced further complexities, such as double rhyme in certain metres, and invented two new measures which interlocked rhyme and *cynghanedd* to the point of absurdity and which were hardly ever used except as exercises or tests for poets at subsequent eisteddfodau. He also brought stricter control over the intricate rules relating to *cynghanedd*. The proposals aroused considerable controversy and there were objections to them from the poets of South Wales, but Dafydd ab Edmwnd succeeded in persuading his fellow bards to accept the modifications.

At about this time, in Glamorgan, the *pencerdd* Gwilym Tew of Llangynwyd was also endeavouring to establish rules for Welsh poetry. He composed an *awdl* containing examples of all the accepted metrical forms, and some that were not acknowledged, and copied a number of manuscripts, including the *Donatus*, the grammar that was studied in the bardic schools.

Gutun Owain, otherwise Gruffudd ap Huw ab Owain, a *pencerdd* who owned considerable lands in the vicinity of Oswestry, is said to have accompanied his teacher, Dafydd ab Edmwnd, to the Carmarthen eisteddfod. He was a recognised genealogist and transcriber of manuscripts, and his Grammar, *Cyfrinach Beirdd Ynys Prydain* (The Secret of the Bards of the Isle of Britain), which he compiled in 1455, contained the rules laid down by Dafydd ab Edmwnd. In a summary of the classification of the metres, he describes as the 'five pillars of Taliesin's song' the measures known as *Toddaid, Gwawdodyn byr, Cyhydedd hir, Cyhydedd fer* and *Rhupunt byr,* and states that they were the best measures in the poetry of Taliesin. Four other measures were later invented, he maintains, namely *Gwawdodyn hir, Cyhydedd nawban, Byr a Thoddaid* and *Clogyrnach.* Then Dafydd Ddu Athro invented three more measures: *Cyrch a Chwta, Hir a Thoddaid* and *Tawddgyrch cadwynog.* He adds that Einion Offeriad conceived the measure known as *Rhupunt hir* and that Dafydd ab Edmwnd invented *Gorchest y beirdd* and *Cadwynfyr.* These assertions cannot be accepted in their entirety, however, as it is known that some of the measures were used from earliest times.

The complication of Grammars culminated in the comprehensive work of Simwnt Fychan, *Pum Llyfr Cerddwriaeth* (The Five Books of Minstrelsy), written in about 1570. This book contains five parts, as its name indicates, one of which deals in detail with the intricacies of *cynghanedd*. Simwnt Fychan, a native of Llanfair Dyffryn Clwyd, was a pupil of Gruffudd Hiraethog, a leading bardic teacher of the sixteenth century, who compiled a Welsh dictionary and a collection of family pedigrees, thus exemplifying the interest in heraldry which was a characteristic of the bards of this period.

There is reason to believe that the bards found the Grammars indigestible, since much of their contents was of no practical use. Verbal instructions therefore continued to be an essential feature in the pursuit of knowledge of the craft of poetry.

The Caerwys Eisteddfodau

In 1523 a number of gentlemen of North Wales obtained a commission from Henry VIII to hold an eisteddfod at Caerwys. The promoters claimed that an eisteddfod had been held in the town previously, late in the eleventh century or early in the twelfth, 'before the prince Gruffudd ap Cynan in person' and referred to Gruffudd's 'Statute' in the proclamation:

> *Let it be known to all gentlemen and common men that an eisteddfod for craftsmen in poetry and music (will be held) within the town of Caerwys in Flintshire the second day of the month of July in the fifteenth year of the crowning of Henry VII before Richard ap Hywel ap Ieuan Fychan Esquier with the collaboration of Sir William Gruffudd and Sir Roger Salusbury and with the personal counsel of Gruffydd ap Ieuan ap Llywelyn Fychan and Tudur Aled, a chaired poet, and many gentlemen and wise men besides in order to bring order and government to the craftsmen in poetic art and their art according to the words of the Statute of Gruffudd ap Cynan, Prince of Gwynedd, namely to certify and confirm master craftsmen and those who were previously awarded a degree and to award (a degree) to whoever deserved it and to give space (of time) to others to learn and meditate as deeply as conscience allows and by the Statute of Prince Gruffudd ap Cynan.*

The purpose of the eisteddfod therefore was 'to bring order and government to the craftsmen in poetic art' and this was to be achieved by distinguishing reputable poets from *clêr y dom* who vied with them for the patronage of the nobility. The patrons, on their part, were in favour of the scheme so as to be rid of the host of inferior itinerant minstrels that plagued them. Richard ap Hywel ap Ieuan Fychan of Mostyn Gloddaeth, who presided, had fought at Bosworth for his kinsman, Henry Tudor, and, by his wife Catherine, daughter of Thomas Salusbury of Llewenni, was father of Thomas Mostyn, the first of the Mostyn family to be known by that name. Richard, and Sir William Gruffydd of Penrhyn (father-in-law of Thomas Mostyn) and Sir Roger Salusbury of Llewenni, sat as commissioners and they were assisted in the grading of poets by Gruffydd ap Ieuan ap Llewelyn Fychan, bard and gentleman, of Llewenni Fechan, and Tudur Aled.

Tudur Aled was born in the parish of Llansannan in Denbighshire of gentle birth. He claimed that he was a pupil of Dafydd ab Edmwnd, an uncle by blood, and of Ieuan ap Llewelyn Fychan, who was present at the marriage feast in the hall of Ieuan ap Dafydd ab Ithel Fychan of Tegeingl at which Tudur had conferred upon him his first degree as a bard. Despite his noble descent, he wandered from court to court and some of his best *cywyddau* are poems of asking, in the traditional manner, such as the *cywydd* requesting a stallion on which he could carry off his ladylove, a stallion of fine appearance:

> Llygaid fal dwy ellygen
> Llymion byw'n llamu'n eu ben;
> Dwyglust feinion aflonydd,
> Dail saets wrth ei dâl y sydd.

(Eyes like two pears, lively and leaping in his head; two slender, restless ears like sage leaves at his forehead).

He was a poet of great distinction and, as an acknowledged chief master craftsman in the craft of poetry, he was in a position to certify and confirm master craftsmen and to award degrees in accordance with the terms of the 'Statute'.

The *Law* of Hywel Dda had referred to three classes of poets — *pencerdd* (chief poet), *bardd teulu* (family poet) and *cerddor* (minstrel), and Einion Offeiriad had named them *prydydd*, *teuluwr* and *clerwr*, but the 'Statute of Gruffudd ap Cynan' classified them according to degrees in greater detail. The lowest order, *disgybl ysbas heb radd* (apprentice for a space of time without a degree) had to serve for a probationary period before he was accepted as a *disgybl ysbas graddol* (apprentice for a time with degree) who had to master six of the twenty-four metres and satisfactorily complete a course 'by the end of three years' before graduating as *disgybl disgyblaidd* (amenable apprentice). He had now to learn twelve of the twenty-four metres and could either stay in this grade or else enter as a *disgybl pencerddaidd* (chief poet's apprentice). By the end of his apprenticeship in this degree he had to master all twenty-four metres and all the mysteries of *cynghanedd* before qualifying as a *pencerdd*, for a *pencerdd* 'should know everything'.

A code of behaviour for bards is also laid down in the 'Statute'. They were not to get drunk at feasts and they were not to go to hidden corners to play dice or cards or any other game for profit. And under no circumstances were they to make unseemly advances to the ladies of the houses they visited.

A poet could receive a degree at the marriage feast of a royal person, or of someone descended from any of the royal tribes, but the 'Statute' recommended that the degree should be received at a 'warranted eisteddfod', and that such an eisteddfod should be held every three years at an appointed place after being proclaimed a year and a day in advance in all the fairs and markets.

The 'Statute' attributed to Gruffudd ap Cynan was undoubtedly compiled before or during the Caerwys Eisteddfod and refers to conditions existing in the sixteenth century rather than in the time of Gruffudd. Likewise, the tradition of an eisteddfod held at Caerwys before Prince Gruffudd ap Cynan in person was probably invented in order to promote the 1523 Eisteddfod.

The silver chair at the Eisteddfod was awarded to Tudur Aled, who was acknowledged as the chief *pencerdd* of Gwynedd. The silver harp for the leading musician went to Dafydd Nantglyn, and degrees, according to their proficiency, were conferred on twelve musicians and an unkown number of poets.

Although the 'Statute' had laid down that eisteddfodau should be held every three years, there is no evidence that another took place until 1567, again at Caerwys. It was held under a royal Commission given at Chester on the twenty-third day of October of the ninth year of her reign by Elizabeth I through the Council of Wales and the Marches:

> Elizabeth by the grace of god of England, ffraunce and Ireland Quene defender of the faythe, &c. To our trustie and right welbeloued Sr Richard Bulkeley knight, Sr Rees Gruffith knight, Ellice Price Esquior doctor in Cyvill Lawe, and one of

our Counsaill in our marches of wales william mostyn, Jeuan lloyd of Yale, John Salusbury of Ruge, Rees Thomas, Maurice wynne, wim Lewis, Peres mostyn, Owen John ap holl vaughan, John wim ap John, John Lewis owen, morris gruffyth, Symound Theloall, John Gruffyth, Ellice ap wm lloyd, Robt Puleston, harry aparry, william Glynne and Rees hughes Esquiors and to euery of them, Greeting.

Whereas it is come to the knowledge of the Lorde President and other our said Cunsaill in our marches of wales that vagrant and idle persons naming theim selfes mynstrelles Rithmers and Barthes, are lately growen into such an intollerable multitude within the principalitee of north wales, that not only gentlemen and other by theire shameles disorders are oftentymes disquieted in theire habitacions / But also thexpert mynstrelles and musicions in tonge and Conyng thereby much discouraged to travail in thexercise and practize of theire knowledges and also not a little hyndred in theire lyvinges and prefermentes. The Refourmacion whereof and the putting of those people in order the said Lorde President and Counsaill have thought verey necessarye and knowing you to be men both of wysdome and vpright dealing and also of Experience and good Knowledge in the scyence / have apounted and aucthorized you to be Commissyoners for that purpose / And forasmuch as our said Counsaill of late travalying in some parte of the said principalite had perfect vnderstanding by credible report that thaccumstomed place for thexecution of the like Commissyon / hath bene heretofore at Cayroes in our Countie of fflynt, and that william mostyn Esquior and his auncestors have had the gyfte and bestowing of the sylver harpe appertayning to the Cheff of that facultie / and that a yeares warning at the least hath bene acustomed to be geaven of thassembly / and execucion of the like Commissyon Our said Counsaill have therefore apoynted thexecucion of this Commissyon to be at the said towne of Cayroes the monday next after the feast of the blessed Trynitee which shall be in the yeare of our Lorde god/1568. And therefore we require and commaund you by the authoritee of these presentes not only to cause open proclamcions to be made in all ffayors, markettes, Townes, and other places of assembly within our Counties of Anglizey, Carnarven, meryonneth, denbigh and fflynt / that all and eury person and persons that entend to maynteigne theire lyvinges by name or Colour of mynstrelles, Rithmers, or Barthes, within the Talaith of Aberfrowe comprehending the said fyve Shires, shalbe and appeare before you the said daye and place to showe furth theire learninges accordingly / But also that you ... repayre to the said place the daye aforesaid / And calling to you such expert men in the said facultie of the welshe musick, as to you shall be thought convenient to proceade thexecucion of the premisses and to admytt such an so many as by your wisdomes and Knowledges you shall fynde worthy into / and under the degrees, ... geaving straight monycion and commandment in our name, and on our behalf to the rest not worthy that they returne to some honest Labour and due Exercise, such as they be most apte vnto for mayntenaunce of theire lyvinges vpon paine to be taken as sturdy and idle vacaboundes and to be vsed according to the Lawes and Statutes provided in that behalf ...

Although the date given in the Commission is 1568, the evidence shows that the eisteddfod was held on 26 May 1567, the first Monday after the feast of the Trinity in that year.

William Mostyn, member of Parliament for Flintshire and three times high sheriff of that county, was the grandson of Richard ap Hywel who had presided over the 1523 Eisteddfod and, as the Commission points out, he 'and his auncestors have had the gyfte and bestowing of the Sylver harpe appertayning to the Cheff of that facultie'. The silver chair, the silver *crwth* for the best fiddler, the silver tongue for the best singer and the silver harp had all to be returned to Mostyn Hall after the ceremony. The silver harp, measuring some six inches in length, is still in the possession of the Mostyn family.

According to one report the chair was won by Simwnt Fychan of Llanfair Dyffryn Clwyd, while another states that it was awarded to William Llyn. They, together with Lewis ab Edward of Bodfari and Owain Gwynedd, all pupils of Gruffudd Hiraethog, were licensed and graduated in the degree of *pencerdd cerdd dafod*. Seven other poets were admitted to the rank of *disgybl pencerdd*, three as *disgyblion disgyblaidd* and three as *disgybl ysbas*. The Commission, it will be recalled, summoned the 'mynstrelles, rithmers or barthes within the Talaith of Aberfrowe', namely the kingdom of the kings of Gwynedd whose throne was at Aberffraw, to appear before the Commissioners 'to show forth their learning'. Those who failed to prove themselves worthy, in the eyes of the Commissioners, were ordered to 'return to some honest labour' failing which they could be charged as 'sturdy and idle vagabonds' and dealt with according to law. Most of the Commissioners were magistrates empowered to sign licences for qualified poets, and also under a duty to administer the law relating to beggars and vagabonds. Poets who failed to obtain a degree at an eisteddfod were therefore relegated to the class of vagabonds and liable to be placed in the stocks or, even worse punishment, to be put to work.

The competence of the gentlemen named in the Commission 'to admit such and so many as by your wisdom and knowledge you shall find worthy into and under the degrees' is open to doubt. Several of them, including William Mostyn, Rhys Gruffydd, Simon Thelwall and Siôn ap William ap Siôn of Ysgeifiog, had either written poetry or adjudicated the work of other poets, and took their task seriously, but some of the others were less zealous. Ieuan Llwyd of Yale spent his time playing cards and Dr Elis Prys of Plas Iolyn openly devoted his attentions to a pretty girl, thus indulging themselves in the very sins against which the bards had been warned in the 'Statute of Gruffudd ap Cynan'.

In 1594 a petition was signed by a number of gentlemen of North Wales seeking another eisteddfod to separate the 'worthier sorte' of bards from the multitude of 'loyterers and drones', to be held at 'a convenient place'. The venue is not mentioned and there is no evidence that the eisteddfod was held, despite the influence of the petitioners, who included Sir John Wynn of Gwydir, Tomos Prys of Plas Iolyn and William Salesbury, translator of the New Testament into Welsh.

In the south, Siôn Mawddwy addressed a poem to George Owen of Henllys, lord of Cemais, appealing to him 'to seek an eisteddfod for those who followed the craft of poetry', but apparently without success.

Even so, the poets continued to compete against each other at bardic gatherings. Such an assembly took place at Llandaff towards the end of the sixteenth century when a group of bards met 'to sing in verse for the mastery'. The adjudicators were Thomas Lewis of Van and William Evans, chancellor and treasurer of that diocese.

There are few detailed accounts of eisteddfodau held during the seventeenth century. Edward Morris, the poet and drover of Perthi Llwydion, Cerrigydrudion, and family bard of Thomas Mostyn of Gloddaeth, refers to an eisteddfod at Bala in 1663 and it is claimed that Siôn Prichard Prys of Llangadwaladr had composed *englynion* at another eisteddfod held in the same town in 1680 in which he sought the aid of Sir Roger Mostyn and the Bishop of Bangor 'to obtain a patent to hold an eisteddfod without delay'.

The Bardic Tradition

The writing of poetry was of the essence of life among the Welsh. Poems were written to mark birth, marriage and death; there were poems to express love or hate, to beg a favour or to grant a boon; there were heroic poems for the brave, flattering poems for those subject to flattery, and satirical or scurrilous poems for the unfortunate or unpopular. Arguments or disputes often resulted in lengthy word battles. An *englyn* sent by Edmund Prys, archdeacon of Merioneth, in 1580 to William Cynwal reminding him that he had promised an archer's bow to Rhys Wyn of Maentwrog resulted in a poetic cut and thrust that lasted over seven years and culminated in a bitter controversy over bardic learning. Cynwal would not recognise Prys as a poet because he had not been reared in the bardic tradition and taunted him: 'Ni raddiwyd dy brydyddiaeth' (Your poetry has not qualified for a degree). According to Cynwal, only those who had been initiated into the mysteries of bardic art and who had graduated in accordance with the rules of the Order of Bards were fit to be recognised as poets, and this typified the attitude of the craftsmen-poets of the period. There were others, however, who spoke against this attitude. Dr Sion Dafydd Rhys, the eminent physician and grammarian, complained that the bards 'kept their art hidden without revealing it to anyone except to some disciple who will swear that he will not teach it to anyone else, or to an occasional gentleman who promises upon his honour to keep it a secret'. He and others of like thought wished to reveal the glory of Welsh poetry 'to the sight of all Europe in a language that was common to all'. But the bards clung to the traditional method of presenting their poems in manuscript to their patrons.

The bards were constantly reminded of their duties and these were laid down once again in a document of the late sixteenth century:

> *The office or function of the British or Cambrian Bards, was to keep and preserve Tri Chôv Ynys Prydain: that is the Three Records, or Memorials, of Britain, otherwise called the British Antiquities ... for the preservation whereof, when the Bards were graduated at their Commencements, they were trebly rewarded:*
> *The First of three Côv is the history of notable acts of the Kings and Princes of Britain and Cambria. The Second of the three Côv is the language of the Britons, of which the Bards were to give an account of every word and syllable therein, when*

*demanded of them; in order to preserve the ancient language,
and to prevent its intermixture with any foreign tongue, or the
introduction of any foreign word in it, to the prejudice of their
own whereby it might be corrupted or extirpated.*
*The Third Côv of the pedigrees, or descents of the nobility,
their division of lands, and blazoning of Arms.*

Many of the early writings were lost during later centuries, in
particular when the monasteries were dissolved and with the loss of
patronage of the nobility. Dr Siôn Dafydd Rhys, in his *Grammar*
published in 1592, refers to their disappearance:

*After the death of their custodians, these books by misfortune
fell into the hands of children who destroyed them and used
them to make toys; or to women shopkeepers to pack vege-
tables; or else to tailors to make patterns for clothes, so that
little of the better things in Welsh survive without being
damaged or destroyed.*

Among those who played an important part in the preservation
of ancient Welsh documents was Robert Vaughan (1592-1667), of
Hengwrt, near Dolgellau, the collector of the famous Hengwrt
library. He was a diligent transcriber of old manuscripts in a
period when such documents were in danger of being lost and it
was he who preserved for us some of our most priceless manuscripts, such as *Llyfr Du Caerfyrddin* (The Black Book of Carmarthen), *Llyfr Taliesin* (The Book of Taliesin), *Llyfr Gwyn
Rhydderch* (The White Book of Rhydderch) which contained the
earliest copy of the *Mabinogi*, and *Llyfr Du'r Waun* (The Black
Book of Chirk) containing the earliest Latin transcript from the
Law of Hywel Dda. This was the finest collection of Welsh manuscripts ever collected by an individual and it remained at Hengwrt
until 1859 when it passed to William Watkin Edward Wynne
(1801-80) of Peniarth, near Towyn. It remained at Peniarth until
1909 when it was purchased by Sir John Williams (1840-1926), the
Court physician and collector of books and manucripts. He presented the Peniarth manuscripts to the newly established National
Library of Wales at Aberystwyth.

The Eighteenth Century

By the end of the seventeenth century, the quality of Welsh
poetry had degenerated considerably. Siôn Richard Prys in his
Difyrrwch Barddonol (The Delight of Poetry) complained that 'the

metres have been shattered, the *cynghaneddau* have been emasculated, the art has languished'. Sion Rhydderch, the grammarian and almanack publisher, bemoaned the fate of the language and its literature and held the view that in the eisteddfod lay the best hope for its salvation. He was associated with the Machynlleth eisteddfod of 1702, held so as 'to begin to revive and bring order to the Eisteddfod of the poets (as it used to be in old times), to reprove false *cynghanedd*, to explain the dark and difficult things, and to verify that which is correct in the art of Poetry in the Welsh language'.

In his *Grammadeg Cymraeg* (Welsh Grammar), published in 1728, he outlined the procedure to be followed at such events, based on the regulations laid down in the 'Statute of Gruffudd ap Cynan' which continued to be accepted as the yardstick:

> When the assembly is gathered, in response to a summons or call, at a particular town or village, they firstly choose twelve men knowledgeable in the Welsh language and also in poetry and in verse. If there will be judges among them, they shall set the subjects for the compositions of the bards, either for an *englyn unodl union* or a *cywydd* or any of the twenty-four measures, but not for a lyric or carol or some poor verse which the chief bards will not as much as acknowledge because there are no established rules attached to them. The adjudicators shall warn the competitors that they must not satire or revile, one the other, and give them time to compose an *englyn* or a *cywydd* as would seem appropriate. The names of competitors are taken so that each may be called by name and in the right order to the Chair to recite his poem. And those who do not win the chair must concede defeat on paper and deliver it to the Chief Bard or to the Chaired Bard, and they must drink the health of the Chief Bard and place six pence each in the cup for him.

The bards were thus encouraged to regard themselves as the upholders of the Welsh literary tradition.

In 1679, Thomas Jones of Tre'r Ddol near Corwen obtained letters patent granting him the sole right of writing, printing and publishing an almanack 'in the British Language'. Jones had spent his early life in London first as a tailor and later as a successful bookseller and publisher before settling in Shrewsbury, in about 1695, and establishing the position of that town as the leading centre for the publication of Welsh books. The first Welsh almanack was published in 1680 and it contained a calendar, a list of fairs, astrological prophecies and a considerable number of poems. Other almanack-makers followed to meet the popular demand for these publications, including Siôn Rhydderch, Gwilym Howel of Llanidloes, and John Prys (Philomath). Much of the poetry published in the almanacks consisted of ballads and light verse, but there were besides the more classical works such as the *cywyddau* of Goronwy Owen and Ieuan Fardd.

The almanacks also proved to be useful media for publicising the eisteddfodau that were being held up and down the country throughout the eighteenth century, so that they gradually became known as *Eisteddfodau'r Almanaciau*. The eisteddfod of this period consisted of a gathering of poets meeting in a tavern or inn to compose extempore verses in competition against each other. The tavern gatherings attracted the scorn of some: William Wynn, the antiquary and vicar of Llanbrynmair, referred to those who frequented them as 'our contemptible set of smatterers in *barddoniaeth* that make a figure in our Welsh almanacs'. Others, like Siôn Rhydderch, travelled all over Wales to attend the meetings in the belief that they were the inheritors of the Caerwys eisteddfodau; and he publicised them in his almanack. In the almanack for 1719 he inserted the following notice:

> *Be it known to all Poets and men of Letters and other merry men of Wales that an Eisteddfod of the Poets of Wales will be held at the Cat Inn, Llandegla-in-Yale in Denbighshire on the 14th day of March 1719.*

That these eisteddfodau were not well-attended is indicated by Siôn Rhydderch's complaint, in the introduction to his almanack of 1735, that an eisteddfod held the previous year at Dolgellau had been a disappointment. He had travelled over eighty miles from Carmarthen, now over sixty years old and in reduced circumstances, greatly hoping 'to have the company of the majority of the Welsh bards, who had some talent in poetry. But not half a dozen came in all'. He saw there 'only signs of apathy, faintheartedness and cowardice' and suspected a deterioration in the craft of poetry since the nobility had withdrawn the patronage it had extended at Caerwys and at other eisteddfodau.

At the eisteddfod held at Cymer on St. David's Day 1735, also attended by no more than half a dozen poets, a poem satirizing the bards was written by Wil Hopcyn, the thatcher-poet from Llangynwyd, who is said to have written *Bugeilio'r Gwenith Gwyn*

(Watching the White Wheat) as a love-poem to Ann Thomas, 'the Maid of Cefn Ydfa'.

The eisteddfod held at Bala on Whit-Monday in 1738 had Edward Wynne, vicar of Gwyddelwern, to preside over its proceedings, and he set the mood by addressing an *englyn* to each of the bards present, which included one woman, Sian Evans of Llanfaircaereinion. The Chair was won by Ellis Cadwaladr of Llandrillo for a poem in praise of Sir Watkin Williams Wynn, and there were eulogistic *englynion* sung to Squire William Price of Rhiwlas and poems in praise of the family of William Lloyd of Rhiwedog.

There was another eisteddfod held at Bala in 1740 and there are accounts of others at Llansanffraid Glyn Ceiriog in 1743, at Selatyn in 1748 and at Llansannan in 1769.

In Philomath's almanack *Dehonglydd y Sêr* (Interpreter of the Stars) for 1759 it was announced that an 'Eisteddfod of the Poets and Musicians of Wales will be held at the Bull in Bala town on Whit-Monday and Whit-Tuesday in 1760'. The announcement proclaims that 'it will be held under the same rules and in the like manner as the ancient Eisteddfod at Caerwys in the days of Queen Elizabeth' and adds that 'at the same time and place there will be an eminent Master of Art (of Poetry) to pass judgement as is the right of a man who has that honourable rank'. In his almanack *Tymhorol Newyddion o'r Wybren* (Seasonal News from the Firmament) for 1773, Gwilym Howell of Llanidloes complained that he had received no support at the eisteddfod which he had arranged in the Red Lion in that town the previous year and wrote: 'In last year's Almanack we invited people to a meeting of Bards at Llanidloes to be held last Whit-Monday. Perhaps some readers wish to know what happened there. Well, only one skilled bard turned up, John Jenkins of Cardigan. Hardly any verse was brought out there that was at all edifying or wise or amusing. Still, to satisfy such Welshmen as want to know about it, we print here a little of that sham poetry, such as it was'.

John Jenkin (Ioan Siengcin) a Cardigan cobbler, was invited by Griffith Jones of Llanddowror in 1754 to open a Welsh school at Nevern in North Pembrokeshire and he continued to be its master for forty years, even though it had become an English school in 1780. He had learned the art of poetry from his father, Siencyn Thomas of Llechryd, and from Siôn Rhydderch's *Grammadeg*, and he addressed many of his poems to his patron Thomas Lloyd of Cwm-gloyn. Despite the disappointment of Llanidloes, he arranged for an eisteddfod to be held at Cardigan in 1773, and he also appears to have been prominent at an eisteddfod held on Whit-Monday, 23 May 1774, 'at the house of John Davies under the sign of the Ship and Castle', at Newport in Pembrokeshire.

The 'almanack eisteddfodau' were rustic affairs held in lowly inns in small country towns, without ceremony and with little preparation. They were, in one sense, national events, to which poets from all over Wales were invited. At the same time, they provided a forum for country poets who wrote verse, much of it in *cynghanedd*, while going about their daily tasks or during their brief leisure. Although they may not have been important in themselves, they served as a medium to keep the eisteddfod alive during a difficult period, thus providing a link between the glory that was Caerwys and the revived eisteddfod which was to emerge under the patronage of the learned societies in London.

Llangollen, 1789 — Caerwys, 1798

On 6 January 1789 an eisteddfod was held at Llangollen to which all the leading bards of north Wales had been invited. According to one report, the instigator was Jonathan Hughes of Pengwern, a sturdy supporter of the earlier eisteddfodau, but it is also claimed that 'the principal mover' was John Edwards of Pen-y-bryn, also near Llangollen, who was reputed to be 'as fond of *barddoniaeth* as of *cwrw* (beer) and *vice versa*'. However, owing to the inclemency of the weather, only two bards appeared, according to Jonathan Hughes, apart from himself and his son Jonathan. But there was a young man present at the gathering who was so impressed by what he saw and heard that he became convinced that the eisteddfod could be used as the medium for the promotion of the arts, and as a means of providing patronage for the bards. His name was Thomas Jones.

Thomas Jones was born near Ruthin, in the parish of Clocaenog, and in 1789 he was an exciseman at Corwen. He was a man of wide interest, in poetry, music and art, and claimed that he had long cherished the idea of developing the eisteddfod as a cultural instrument.

Despite the disappointing attendance, the Llangollen eisteddfod is memorable because of the decision by its promoters to seek the support of the learned societies which had been founded by prominent Welshmen in London, notably the Honourable Society of Cymmrodorion and the Gwyneddigion Society.

The Cymmrodorion Society had been established in September 1751 under the patronage of Frederick, Prince of Wales. Its promoter was Richard Morris who had left his native Llanfihangel-tre'r-beirdd in Anglesey at the age of eighteen to become a clerk in a London office, and later chief clerk for Foreign Accounts to the Comptroller of the Navy. He was an active member of the Society of Ancient Britons and became the first President of the Cymmrodorion — a name suggested by his brother, Lewis Morris, to signify 'the original inhabitants'.

The Gwyneddigion Society was founded by two officials of the Cymmrodorion, Owen Jones (Owain Myfyr) its Assistant Secretary, and Robert Hughes (Robin Ddu o Fôn) its Librarian, in December 1770. The Cymmrodorion Society became defunct, for a time, in 1787 and the Gwyneddigion assumed its role as the chief patron of Welsh learning.

It was to the Gwyneddigion, therefore, that Jonathan Hughes wrote to ask for a prize to be awarded at the eisteddfod that was to be held at Corwen in the following May which, he assured the Society, would receive the support of the gentlemen and clergy of Merioneth. Thomas Jones also wrote, as the promoter of the Corwen eisteddfod, asking for advice as he wished to 'do the thing well', and he received a lengthy and encouraging reply from the Secretary, William Owen Pughe, expressing agreement with the view that the most effective way of providing assistance for the bards would be achieved by promoting the eisteddfod, and pledging the Society's support. The Society would offer a chair and medals on condition that the chief prize would be awarded for the best 'heroic poem', the subject of which would be announced in advance at the time of the proclamation of the eisteddfod, and entries submitted under a nom-de-plume and adjudicated before the event. This would not preclude the bards from pursuing their *englyn*-writing competitions on extemporaneous subjects but these would take second place and would not be the main feature as they had been at the earlier eisteddfodau. The winner of the chief prize would be hailed as the *pencerdd* of the eisteddfod, and the poet who received the award in the impromptu competition would be given the rank of *disgybl pencerddaidd*.

The Society was unable to provide the prizes for the eisteddfod that Thomas Jones had planned to be held at the Owain Glyndŵr Hotel at Corwen on 12 May 1789, as the notice was too short, but he nevertheless announced that the event was being held under the patronage of the Gwyneddigion. At his own expense, he publicised the event in the Shrewsbury and Chester newspapers, which were the newspapers circulating North Wales, and sent a broadsheet to the gentry, clergy and ministers and to bards and musicians, and he also met the cost of the arrangements at the Owain Glyndŵr. Sir

Robert Williams Vaughan of Nannau gave, as the prize for the successful bard, a silver breastplate bearing the figure of a harp, and Edward Jones, harpist to the Prince of Wales, who became known as *Bardd y Brenin* (the king's bard) on the accession of George IV, offered a silver medal for the best singer with the harp. Thomas Jones is alleged to have given Gwallter Mechain advance notice of the 'spontaneous' subjects set for the various competitions, thus giving him a great advantage over the other eight bards competing at Corwen. Even so, the adjudicators failed to choose between his poem and those of Twm o'r Nant and Jonathan Hughes, and the entries were sent to London for adjudication by the Gwyneddigion. The Society was divided between those who favoured the work of Gwallter Mechain and the supporters of Twm o'r Nant, but finally decided in favour of the former. One of the prominent Gwyneddigion, David Samwell, the naval surgeon and poet, felt that Twm should have received the award and sent him a silver writing-pen as a consolation prize.

This dissension led to a correspondence in the press which gave the eisteddfod movement considerable publicity, and Thomas Jones was glad to be able to say that 'the Eisteddfod is now become a topical discourse in most company here'. It was also the means whereby the Society of Gwyneddigion became involved in eisteddfodau in Wales.

Thomas Jones lost no time in preparing for another eisteddfod, to be held at Bala at Michaelmas in the same year. He now had the full support of the Gwyneddigion Society, which undertook to promote the event under its own control and at its own expense, and this it was able to do on account of the generosity of Owain Myfyr, a native of Llanfihangel Glyn Myfyr who had amassed a fortune as a skinner in London, and had been the guiding force behind the Society for over twenty years. Owain Myfyr regarded the eisteddfod as a forum for the political aim of the Society, which he had defined as 'Liberty in Church and State', and he was influential in choosing the subjects set for competition at subsequent eisteddfodau.

The bards were invited to compose an *awdl* on *Ystyriaeth ar Oes Dyn* (Meditation on the Life of Man) and the twelve entries submitted had to be sent to London for adjudication. The Gwyneddigion were not slow to show their disappointment with the entries, which were of the illustrative type containing examples of each of the twenty-four metres laid down by Dafydd ab Edmwnd. The Gwyneddigion set their standards by the works of Goronwy Owen (1723-69) and his critical hypothesis on the nature of poetry, which strongly opposed the proliferation of Welsh metres. They published their adjudication on the twelve entries submitted, and in reiterating their views on poetic composition, they urged the bards to renounce several of the traditional metres.

The eisteddfod was held at the Town Hall at Bala and the bards and musicians were admitted without charge. On the wall, above the place where they sat, hung a painting by Thomas Jones of the Muse weeping over the three poets whose work had caused such disagreement at Corwen in May. But the idea did not amuse those present, and it was not received well by the Gwyneddigion when Jones sent it to them at a later date, as a present. Thomas Jones opened the proceedings by reading the adjudication, dealing only with the work of *Anonymous*, the nom-de-plume of Gwallter Mechain. Members of the Society had again argued between his entry and the one submitted by Twm o'r Nant and had finally chosen in favour of Gwallter Mechain. This did not meet with the approval of the bards present at the eisteddfod and they walked out during the chairing ceremony, but the gathered assembly drank the chaired bard's 'health three times three' in the manner that had been customary at the tavern eisteddfodau.

The Society was represented at the eisteddfod by Siôn Goch (John Hughes), a solicitor who hailed from Denbigh, and Siôn Penllyn (John Williams), a Captain and Paymaster of the 2nd Battalion of the 73rd Regiment of Foot, who later complained to the Society that the event was 'conducted rather void of the form and regularity it requires' and expressed his disapproval of the heavy drinking and excessive noise.

The bards spent the rest of the day and the next morning composing *englynion* on set subjects before the adjudicators awarded the prize to Dafydd Ddu Eryri. The compositions of the sixteen bards present at the eisteddfod were published in a separate volume, rather than in the almanacks, by Thomas Jones, under the title *Gorchestwaith Beirdd Cymru yr Oes Bresennol yn Eisteddfod y Bala* (Masterly Work of the Welsh Bards of the Present Age at the Bala Eisteddfod). There were eleven singers and four harpists competing in the musical competitions. Edward Jones (Bardd y Brenin) gave a medal for the best collection of *penillion* (traditional verses), a new competition in the history of the eisteddfod, and the three competitors, between them, produced 730 verses, most of which later appeared in the second edition of Edward Jones's *Musical and Poetical Relicks*. Siôn Penllyn, in his report on the eisteddfod, stated that the singers 'sang incessantly till the evening following, till our Welsh Garrick, Twm o'r Nant, entertained the Town with an *anterliwt* (interlude) and continued for two or three days longer'.

The importance of the Bala Eisteddfod was out of all proportion to its size. For the first time the general public was admitted to an eisteddfod — on presentation of a ticket bearing the legend *Publica concordia nihil utilus*. For the first time, the subject set for the *awdl* was announced in advance, and, for the first time, a drama in the form of an *anterliwt*, was performed while an eisteddfod was in session.

The second eisteddfod sponsored by the Society of Gwyneddigion was held at St. Asaph in 1790, at the Rose Inn. Dafydd Ddu Eryri won the medal offered by the Society for an *awdl* on *Rhyddid* (Freedom), the subject chosen by Owain Myfyr to propogate the Society's political Radicalism. He had been wise enough to abandon the old illustrative type of *awdl* and to concentrate on the metres favoured by the Gwyneddigion.

Dafydd Ddu was a schoolmaster who regarded the eisteddfod as a training centre for the bards. He deplored the tendency for it to become a competitive meeting without devoting time for the compositions to be discussed. He therefore established literary societies, such as *Cymdeithas yr Eryron* (the Society of Eagles), founded at Betws Garmon but later moved to Caernarfon, and the *Cymreigyddion Bangor*, and organised eisteddfodau associated with them at which there were ample opportunities for discussion and criticism of the compositions, as well as instruction in the poetic arts. He had inherited the poetical and critical standards of Goronwy Owen and believed that Welsh poets should be given more freedom but that 'this freedom should be sparingly used lest a way should be opened for unworthy rhymesters to break into the realm of poetry'. As a result of his teaching there arose a school of bards, referred to as *cywion Dafydd Ddu* (Dafydd Ddu's chickens) which included Gutyn Peris (Griffith Williams), Gwilym Peris (William Williams), Gwyndaf Eryri (Richard Jones), Gwilym Padarn (William Edwards), Ieuan Lleyn (Evan Pritchard) and Cawrdaf (William Ellis Jones).

At the Llanrwst Eisteddfod, held on 14 and 15 September 1791, Dafydd Ddu won the medal for his *awdl* on *Gwirionedd* (Truth). *Englynion* composed by Jonathan Hughes to welcome the eisteddfod to the town contain the oft-quoted invitation:

Dwy ochr y wlad dewch i'r wledd
(Both ends of the land, come to the feast).

The eisteddfod held at Denbigh in the following year appears to have reverted to tavern standards and a contemporary critic opined that Bacchus, and not the Muse, had taken possession of the minds of the bards.

Bala was the venue once more in 1793 but, by that time, a religious revival had taken a hold on the town — 'a very great and powerful and glorious overpowering of the spirit on the people', according to Thomas Charles. He felt that 'this revival of religion has put an end to all the merry meetings for dancing, singing with the harp, and every kind of sinful mirth... No harps but the golden harps which St. John speaks of have been played in this neighbourhood for several months past'. The Eisteddfod suffered on account of this piety and Thomas Jones maintained that it had been folly to hold it 'among the saints of Bala'.

Two chairs were offered at Dolgellau in the following year, one for the bard who won the Society's medal for the *awdl*, and the other for the poet who was declared the winner in the impromptu competition.

Dafydd Ddu Eryri was invited by the Gwyneddigion to organise the 1795 Eisteddfod at Penmorfa, near Dolbenmaen. Thomas Jones by this time had been posted to Somerset and had, to his immense sorrow, to sever his connection with Wales and the eisteddfod.

In 1798 the eisteddfod returned to Caerwys and the notice published by the Gwyneddigion Society and dated 'Whitsun 1797' announced:

> Be it known to the Bards, Harpists and Singers that an Eisteddfod will be held during Whitsun in the year 1798, namely after notice of one year and a day, and in the old Hall, by request of, and at the expense of the Society of Gwyneddigion in London, under the guidance of the Reverend gentlemen Robert Thomas, Peter Whitley, Robert Williams, Llywelyn Llwyd and Walter Davies, and also Dafydd Ddu Eryri, Chaired Bard, and many others of the sages of Wales. The Subject: *Cariad i'n Gwlad drwy Adgyfodiad yr Hen Eisteddfod a Defodau Cymru* (Love of Our Country by Resurrection of the Old Eisteddfod and the Customs of Wales). *Note* — The Bards, Harpists and Soloists will receive awards according to their grade, and merit. The Hall will be opened on Whit-Tuesday, 1798. The Bards should send their work to the Reverend Mr. Llwyd of Caerwys about a month before the meeting. The remarkable hall mentioned above is the place where the magnificent Eisteddfod, by command of the Queen Elisabeth, was held in the year 1567.

There follows a poem of exhortation which includes the significant couplet:

> Dowch chwithau a'ch hymnau heirdd,
> Ddiwair, addfwyn Dderwyddfeirdd

(Come also, with your beautiful hymns, ye chaste and gentle Druid-bards).

Iolo Morganwg

Throughout the eighteenth century, there was a growing interest in Welsh antiquities. Edward Lhuyd, keeper of the Ashmolean Museum, published his epoch-making *Archaeologica Britannica* in 1707, which laid the foundation for all subsequent studies of the Celtic language. In 1716, Theophilus Evans (1693-1767) published *Drych y Prif Oesoedd* (Mirror of the First Ages) in which he claimed an august ancestry for his people based on Geoffrey of Monmouth's *Historia Regum Britanniae*. Written in 1136 it traced the lineage of the Welsh to Gomer (hence 'Cymro'!) son of Japheth son of Noah.

At about the same time the English antiquary William Stukeley began his study of Stonehenge and depicted it as 'the temple of the white-haired Druid bard sublime'. In 1723, Henry Rowland published his *Mona Antiqua Restaurata* in Dublin, describing Anglesey as the home of the Druids in Wales.

By the middle of the century, great efforts were being made to collect and copy medieval Welsh manuscripts, largely under the inspiration of the Society of Cymmrodorion, and of the three Anglesey brothers Lewis, Richard and William Morris, and the circle of poets and scholars they had gathered around them, including Goronwy Owen (1723-69) and Ieuan Fardd (1731-88). In 1764, Ieuan Fardd published *Some Specimens of the Poetry of the Ancient Welsh Bards* which created an interest among English antiquaries in early Welsh literature.

It was in the atmosphere of this romantic movement that the Glamorgan poet and scholar, Edward Williams (Iolo Morganwg) conceived the notion of attaching druidical origins to Welsh bardism and, in 1785, he wrote a letter to *The Gentlemen's Magazine* which contained a reference to *Cyfrinach Beirdd Ynys Prydain* (The Mystery of the Bards of the Isle of Britain).

Edward Williams was born in the village of Pennon in the parish of Llancarfan in Glamorgan on 10 March 1747 but, while he was still young, his parents moved to the neighbouring village of

Flimston. He received no schooling and claimed that he learned to read by watching his father cut the names of the dead on tombstones. He followed his father's trade as a stonemason and, after journeying in North Wales between 1771 and 1773, he went to London and Kent where he worked at his craft for four years before returning to Glamorgan. In 1781 he married and settled at Llandaff and later at Rumney. In 1787 he served a term in Cardiff prison after which he returned to Flimston. By 1791 he was back in London where he spent most of the next four years.

Despite his lack of formal education, Iolo amassed an enormous amount of learning and became versed in theology, geology, botany, horticulture, agriculture, music, politics, architecture and industrial development. He is still regarded as a leading scholar of the period in Welsh history and literature, and a considerable romantic poet in the tradition of Dafydd ap Gwilym.

He had been taught the elements of prosody by another Edward Williams, the bard from Llancarfan, and by other Glamorgan poets, including Lewis Hopcyn, the carpenter from Peterston-super-montem, and John Bradford, weaver and dyer from Betws Tir Iarll. In Lewis Hopcyn, Iolo had a tutor in whom rested a long continuity of the bardic tradition. Hopcyn had been taught by pupils of Edward Dafydd of Margam, possibly the last of the professional bards of Glamorgan, who had himself been taught by Llywelyn Siôn, farmer, beadle, and leading literary figure, a contemporary of the pupils of Lewys Morgannwg, grandson of Rhys Brydydd, the fifteenth century poet.

Iolo claimed that he had found in the manuscripts of John Bradford, after his death, evidence of druidic ceremonies being observed for centuries in Glamorgan and particularly in Tir Iarll. He maintained that the bards of Glamorgan had not accepted Dafydd ab Edmwnd's arrangement of the twenty-four metres and had adhered to the ancient measures preserved in Tir Iarll since druidic times. They had kept the eisteddfodau going in the traditional manner and had preserved the druidic succession unbroken from pre-Christian times. It was to promote this theory that Iolo devised a system of bardic metres which he supported with examples allegedly drawn from the works of the early poets, but which were invariably written by him.

When Owain Myfyr and William Owen Pughe were collecting the works of Dafydd ap Gwilym, for publication by the Society of Gwyneddigion in 1789, Iolo sent them a collection of *cywyddau* which he attributed to Dafydd and which he said he had found among ancient manuscripts in Glamorgan. These were accepted by the Gwyneddigion and by Welsh scholars for a century and more, before it was realised that most of them had been written by Iolo.

The vogue in medievalism and the researches into early literature had led to the publication of some spurious works. Thomas Chatterton had hoaxed his native city of Bristol and had deceived Horace Walpole and the Lord Mayor of London in 1770 with his forgeries taken 'from ancient manuscripts' before consuming a fatal dose of arsenic at the age of seventeen. In Scotland, James Macpherson's 'translation' of the Gaelic poems of the third century warrior-poet Ossian, son of Fingal MacCumhail, had deluded the Faculty of Advocates into sending him into the Highlands to collect more, without suspecting that they were his own invention. Iolo likewise assigned to an obscure poet, Rhys Goch ap Rhiccert, a number of poems of a high order that he himself had written, thus elevating him from a humble position as a poet, and describing him as a forerunner of Dafydd ap Gwilym.

Iolo completely immersed himself in druidic theories and inventions and re-wrote the 'Statute of Gruffudd ap Cynan'. He interpreted an *englyn* which Sils ap Siôn had written at a gathering of bards at Llandaff before Chancellor William Evans and Thomas Lewis of Van, and which contained the line—

i gany ar wawd am y vaistrolaeth
(to sing in verse for the mastery),

as a reference to the traditional eisteddfod of Morgannwg. He maintained that the Chancellor was a generous patron of the arts and that he had established a 'chair' at Llandaff in 1558 for an eisteddfod to be held there each year on the feast of St. Teilo, and claimed that the eisteddfod of Sils ap Siôn's *englyn* was held in 1564.

He wrote accounts of numerous eisteddfodau, *cadeiriau* (chairs) and *gorseddau* (thrones) held in places of Christian worship, such as Llandaff Cathedral, Neath Abbey and the monastery at Penrhys and, in the open air, preferably on the hill tops of Glamorgan — on Garth Mountain at Pentyrch, on Bryn Owen in the vale of Glamorgan, on Twmpath Diwlith on Mynydd Margam, and at Ystrad Owen near Cowbridge which was 'the Bryn Gwyddon of the bardic tradition' and near which a *gorsedd* could be seen. The eisteddfodau had been held by the bards of Glamorgan so as to 'discipline the bardic orders and regulate the poetic metres', and had culminated in the great eisteddfod of Beauprê held under the patronage of Sir Richard Bassett at Whitsun in 1681, at which the Glamorgan classification of the metres had been firmly set out.

Iolo invented his own bardic vocabulary. The chief poet, *pencerdd*, he called *athraw cadeiriog* (chaired teacher) and he used *cadair* (chair) to indicate a provincial eisteddfod and referred to Cadair Morgannwg, Cadair Tir Iarll, Cadair Deheubarth, Cadair Powys and Cadair Gwynedd. The ceremony itself he termed *gorsedd* and he maintained that *gorseddau* were held regularly in Glamorgan at the equinox or solstice — Gorsedd Alban Hefin (Gorsedd of the summer solstice) held on Garth Mountain in 1793, and Gorsedd Gyfallwy'r Alban Elfed (the competent Gorsedd of the autumn equinox) held at Stalling Down in 1798.

In 1791 Iolo returned to London where he stayed until 1795. He began to explain his doctrines on druidism to members of the Society of Gwyneddigion, to whom he revealed the secrets of its mystic rites, and succeeded in enlisting their support in arranging a Gorsedd ceremony on Primrose Hill in London at Alban Hefin, the summer solstice, in 1792. We are told that a circle of stones was formed 'in the middle of which was the Maen Gorsedd or altar, on which a naked sword being placed, all the Bards assisted to sheathe it'; that the bards held 'all their meetings or *Gorseddau* in the open air, on a conspicuous place, whilst the sun was above the horizon', and that 'at these *Gorseddau* it was absolutely necessary to recite the Bardic Traditions'. They were held, Dafydd Ddu Eryri wrote at the time, 'er rhoddi Barn Gorsedd, yn Llygad Haul, ac yn wyneb y Goleuni, ar bawb o barth Awen a Chynneddf' (so as to give a Gorsedd's judgement, in the eye of the sun and in the face of light, upon everyone concerning Muse and Faculty). A second Gorsedd ceremony was held on Primrose Hill at Alban Elfed, the autumn equinox, on 22 September in the same year.

While he was in London, Iolo came into contact with men who sympathised with the French Revolution, and members of the Gwyneddigion who were imbued with ideas of Liberty. Iolo had also met Unitarian leaders and was later to become a zealous promoter of Unitarianism in South Wales. The authorities suspected the Primrose Hill ceremonies of the pacifism that had arisen as a result of the war with France: it may be that Iolo's declared position as a pacifist and the introduction of the ceremony of sheathing the sword led them to this conclusion. In consequence, Iolo was prevented from holding any further ceremonies in London and from 1792 onward he had to confine his activities to Glamorgan and to Wales.

In North Wales, Dafydd Ddu Eryri was in correspondence with

Iolo and with other members of the Gwyneddigion Society. On 13 September 1791, a week before the second ceremony held on Primrose Hill, he wrote a letter to Siôn Lleyn stating: 'I have received three letters from London, one from Gwilym Owain, one from Owain Myfyr and the other from Iolo Morganwg. Iolo is in possession of a book called *Cyfrinach Y Beirdd* which has been in existence since the time of the Druids. There is no one in Wales, save two or three bards, familiar with the secret and it can not be revealed without breaking the most holy laws, a system not unlike that of the Freemasons which is related to it. I am likely to be ordained a bard of the provinces of Glamorgan, Gwent, Ewyas Erging and Powys, that is a member of the mystery the world knows not of. There is no one in Gwynedd who is a bard *by privilege and custom,* and this privilege is not to be awarded to anyone save me, because there is no one else possessed of the necessary faculties (so they say)!' He complained that Gwynedd was bereft of bards ordained in accordance with the customs and privileges, and maintained that not more than one or two people in the whole of Wales would be familiar with the secrets of *Barddas* (poetry). This may be a reference to a statement by Iolo that only he and one other poet, Edward Evans of Aberdare, remained as ordained bards and members of *Gorsedd Beirdd Ynys Prydain.*

In a further letter addressed to Siôn Lleyn on 14 January 1800 Dafydd Ddu wrote: 'You will know that an Eisteddfod was held, in accordance with the custom of the Bards of the Isle of Britain, at Pen Bryn in Arfon, on 16 October 1799, where Ieuan Lleyn, Gutyn Peris and Dafydd Ddu were enrolled and graduated as bards of the Chair of Gwynedd. It is a secret and yet not a secret. I know that you would like to be a member and this you shall be if you live until the Tuesday following next Whitsun, when it is planned to hold an Eisteddfod on Dinorwig Hill, near Llanddeiniolen in Arfon, to meet in the morning at high noon'.

Despite his enthusiasm, Dafydd Ddu parted company with Iolo and with the Gwyneddigion Society seven years later.

Professor Griffith John Williams, the leading authority on Iolo's life and on the literary traditions of Glamorgan, maintained that Iolo's inventions had a profound influence, not only on the history of the eisteddfod but also on the development of national consciousness in the first half of the nineteenth century. Professor Williams ruthlessly exposed the falsehood and the forgery in Iolo's theories but at the same time he admitted that 'behind the fiction may be seen a man of genius, one of the most gifted men in the long history of the Welsh nation'. He pointed out that no man could have created the fiction unless he knew more about the history of Welsh literature and about the content of old Welsh manuscripts than any of his contemporaries. Iolo was 'the first to treat the bardic system intelligently and to make a detailed study of manuscripts such as the Statute of Gruffudd ap Cynan and the old Grammars and the Triads, and it was this knowledge that formed the basis of the Druidic system'.

The eisteddfod, up to the time of Iolo, was merely a gathering of poets and musicians meeting for the purpose of bringing order and discipline into the bardic orders. Apart from the 'special feast' at Cardigan castle, the only eisteddfodau of any consequence had been the one held at Carmarthen *c*. 1451 and those of Caerwys in 1523 and 1567.

Iolo's immediate ambition was to 're-establish' the eisteddfod of the kingdom of Glamorgan under the patronage of the lords of Morgannwg, and it is clear that his views had a considerable influence on his contemporaries in that part of the country, among them the poet and important literary figure Gwilym Morgannwg, author of *Llais Awen Gwent a Morgannwg* (The Voice of the Muse of Gwent and Morgannwg) and *Awenyddion Morgannwg, neu Farddoniaeth Cadair a Gorsedd Pendefigaeth Morgannwg a Gwent* (The Muses of Glamorgan, or the Poetry of the Chair and Gorsedd of the Princedom of Glamorgan and Gwent). Iolo's son, Taliesin ab Iolo, states that Gwilym and he 'were initiated into the arcana of Druidism by my father'. Gwilym was present at the Gorsedd of Morgannwg held 'at the Summer Solstice, in the year 1814', where he declaimed his poem *Heddwch* (Peace) from the Logan Stone, and his was the best *awdl* on the destruction of Caerphilly Castle at the 'fifth eisteddfod held on the day of the Feast of the Summer Solstice, 1825'.

Iolo became so obsessed with his druidic theories that he set out to link everything associated with the past in Wales to the bardic tradition, and he re-wrote and embellished Welsh history accordingly.

He journeyed through North Wales in 1799, visiting Hengwrt and other historic houses, to collect material for *The Myvyrian Archaiology of Wales,* the first collection of early Welsh manuscripts ever to be published. This grandiose task was undertaken by the Gwyneddigion Society under the joint editorship of Owain Myfyr, who met the considerable cost, William Owen Pughe and Iolo, and a nominal committee which included Richard Fenton and Gwallter Mechain. The first volume, published in 1801 and containing the works of the pre-1282 poets, became an authoritative work of reference, but the second and third volumes were bedevilled by Iolo's own interpretation of the Welsh chronicles.

Iolo published but little of his own work and seemed satisfied to inject his own inventions into the publications of the Gwyneddigion Society. His elegy to his bardic teacher, Lewis Hopcyn, was published in 1772 under the title *Dagrau yr Awen* (The Tears of the Muse) and two volumes of his English poems, *Poems Lyrics and Pastoral* were published, and a volume of hymns. His *Cyfrinach Beirdd Ynys Prydain* was published after his death by his son, Taliesin ab Iolo, who also collected a selection of his father's papers which were published by the Welsh MSS Society in 1848 under the title *Iolo Manuscripts*.

For Iolo, the ceremonies on Primrose Hill were great achievements: the Gorsedd of Bards of the Isle of Britain had been firmly re-established, but fulfilment would only be achieved when *Gorsedd y Beirdd* took over the Eisteddfod. He regarded the *Gorsedd* as the academy of the Welsh people, at which poets could graduate with the degree of a B.B.D., *Bardd Braint a Defod* (Bard by Privilege and Custom), which he held to be superior to a degree at Oxford or Cambridge!

Iolo now concentrated on promoting the eisteddfod, with its 'druidic' background, as the focal point of Welsh cultural life, and as the great national institution of the Welsh people. The measure of his achievement is indicated by his sternest critic's confession that 'he gave a cultural focus to the nation'.

The Cambrian Societies

Although the eisteddfod had moved into a new phase under the patronage of the Society of Gwyneddigion it still had not captured the imagination of the people, nor was it showing signs of growth and development as the nineteenth century progressed, and it might well have perished had it not been for the rise of cultural societies, known as Cambrian Societies, in the four ancient kingdoms of Wales. These societies were formed by a group of clergymen with the active support of Dr Thomas Burgess, Bishop of St. David's.

Burgess was born in Hampshire in 1756, and educated at Winchester and Oxford. Since his appointment to the see in 1803 he had shown considerable interest in Welsh life and letters and had felt the need to raise the educational standard of the clergy. For that purpose he had licensed four grammar schools and, in 1821, he laid the foundation stone of St. David's College, Lampeter. He insisted that applicants for incumbencies in his own diocese should be able to speak Welsh, and among these were to be found the group of clerical *literati* who promoted the Cambrian Societies, including John Jenkins (Ifor Ceri), Walter Davies (Gwallter Mechain), David Rowland (Dewi Brefi) and W. J. Rees.

Ifor Ceri, a native of Llangoedmor, had served as a chaplain in the navy, after graduating at Oxford, and had returned as rector of Manordeifi before he was offered the living of Kerry by Bishop Burgess. Here he built a new parsonage and kept open house during the first week of every year for poets and musicians and 'all comers provided only that they could compose an *englyn*, sing a song, or play the harp'. The vicarage became known as *llys Ifor Hael o Ceri* on an analogy with the generous patron of Dafydd ap Gwilym and it is apparent from correspondence between members of the group that such meetings were referred to as 'clerical eisteddfodau'. At one of these gatherings, in January 1818, David Rowland, a native of Llanddewibrefi, who had been licensed to the curacy of St. Peter's, Carmarthen, after serving as a missionary in Newfoundland, suggested that means should be found 'to teach prosody to the clergy'. In this way, he felt, 'bardism may be revived in South Wales, and a new era formed', and he repeated the suggestion to the bishop.

The bishop made a visit to Kerry in order to discuss with Ifor Ceri and Gwallter Mechain, who was vicar of Manafon in the same county, the idea of promoting provincial societies, and to 'make an attempt to rekindle the bardic skill and ingenuity of the Principality by holding eisteddfodau in different places in the four provinces'.

The important part played by Bishop Burgess is emphasized by Ifor Ceri in a letter which he wrote to W. J. Rees, vicar of Cascob in Radnorshire: 'When you speak of the origin of the Cambrian Societies, you ought carefully to avoid taking the credit of it from the Bishop . . . The first suggestion was certainly that of (David) Rowland at Kerry in January 1818, which he shortly afterwards communicated to the Bishop. No notice was taken of it at the time, but when the Bishop came to Kerry in the following August, he was most intent on a plan of that nature, and in travelling towards the Hay reduced it into form and fixed on the name of the Cambrian Society'.

The Nonconformists looked upon the activities of the bishop and his clergy with some suspicion as a stratagem for improving the position of the Church. Despite the Anglican sponsorship, however, it was stressed that 'all Dissenters from the Church who are natives of the Principality and are distinguished as authors of creditable works of literature and religion, may be honorary members of the Society', and its membership included numerous Nonconformist ministers and laymen.

At a meeting held at Carmarthen on 28 October 1818, the Cambrian Society of Dyfed was formed under the patronage of Lord Dynevor, descendant of Gruffudd ap Nicolas, the patron of the Carmarthen Eisteddfod of 1451. On the following day the promoters met again at the Bishop's Palace at Abergwili and decided to establish similar societies in Gwynedd, Powys and Gwent, and to hold eisteddfodau quadrennially in each of the four provinces. Iolo Morganwg, who was present, suggested that the surplus money from these eisteddfodau should be accumulated so that, on the fifth year, 'a grand Gorsedd' could be held in London, but this suggestion did not find favour. Everyone regretted the absence of Gwallter Mechain, who was the most scholarly and influential member of the group; and Ifor Ceri, ignoring Iolo's ability, commented that there was no one present who 'was acquainted in any tolerable degree with the Construction and Rules of Welsh Poetry' except Eliezer Williams, the vicar of Lampeter and son of the Biblical annotator Peter Williams. 'He was too shy to offer his sentiments, though he trembled at the idea of any innovations', such as the suggested abolition of some of the metrical forms and of *cynghanedd* from the competitions, which 'would certainly alarm the Bards and make them believe that the Society intended under cover to barbarize and not preserve the National language'. Dewi Brefi was appointed secretary and the first eisteddfod to be held under the patronage of the Society was proclaimed. A pamphlet was published listing the subjects of the various competitions:

> The following prizes are proposed by the Cambrian Society for the year 1819, viz. Five Guineas for the best *Englyn* on 'The Harp New Strung'; Ten Guineas for the best *Awdl* on the 'Death of Queen Charlotte', and Twenty Guineas or a medal of not less than twenty guineas for the best poem in any one of all the four and twenty metres on 'The Death of Sir Thomas Picton'. Also Ten Guineas for the best English essay on each of the following subjects, viz.

> I. On the Language and Learning of Britain under the Roman Government, with a particular reference to the testimony of Martial *(Dicitur et nostros castare Britannia versus)* and Juvenal and to the influence of Agricola's Schools.

47

II. On the Distinct Characters and Comparative Advantages of the Bardic Institutions of Carmarthen and Glamorgan and on the Notices which remain of each.

Also a Silver Harp will be given with a gratuity to the best proficient on the Harp and other gratuities to the several competitors to defray their expenses.

The Verses and Essays to be delivered into the Secretary, at the Vicarage, Carmarthen, on or before the 1st May, 1819, on or before which day the candidates for the Silver Harp must send their names to the Secretary.

Carmarthen, 1819

The eisteddfod was held in the Ivy Bush Inn, Carmarthen, and lasted from the morning of Thursday, 8 July, 1819, to the following Saturday. Lord Dynevor was unable to preside over the opening session and his place was taken by Bishop Burgess. Between two and three hundred bards, musicians and others attended altogether and the proceedings were carried out with considerable dignity. The *Carmarthen Journal* reported that 'the General Meeting of the members of the newly instituted Cambrian Society commenced with the sound of the trumpet at the Great Room of the Ivy Bush Inn when several prizes were awarded to the successful candidates'. The prize for the *englyn* went to Gwallter Mechain and he was also awarded the prizes for the best essay on the Bardic Institution and for the poem to the memory of General Picton.

Gwallter Mechain was led to a chair, made of oak and fashioned in the Gothic style, that stood on a table in the centre of the Great Room. No sooner was he seated than 'that learned and venerable bard, Mr Edward Williams' (Iolo Morganwg), despite his seventy-two years, leapt on to the table and tied a blue ribbon round the poet's right arm to indicate that he had been admitted a member of the Gorsedd of Bards of the Isle of Britain. Iolo then approached the bishop whom he invested with the order of Druid by knotting a white ribbon on his arm.

The successful competitors read their poems and essays to the assembled company and four harpists 'sang sweet songs between the readings'. Thomas Blayney, harpist to the Earl of Powis, won the Silver Harp and he was paid 30 guineas for his services as *prif delynor* (chief harpist) at the eisteddfod.

On the morning of Saturday, 10 July, a ceremony was held in the garden of the Ivy Bush in order to confer degrees of proficiency on deserving poets. A contemporary report in *Seren Gomer* states that there were present:

eight Bards constituted by privilege and custom — Edward Williams (Iolo Morganwg), Rev. Walter Davies (Gwallter Mechain), Eliezer Williams, Rev. David Richards (Dewi Silin), Rev. Dan Evans (Daniel Ddu o Geredigion), Thomas Williams (Gwilym Morgannwg), Robert Davies (Bardd Nantglyn) and Taliesin Williams (Taliesin ab Iolo). They chose Mr Edward Williams to be the Officiating Bard, and he commenced the ceremony by marking out a circle with small stones placing a large one in the centre, and none but admitted bards would presume to enter the circle. Iolo then took a sheathed sword from the Sword Bearer, Gwilym Morgannwg, and this was unsheathed by the several bards standing within the circle, each one of them at the same time laying a hand on the hilt of the sword and the Officiating Bard holding the point of the scabbard. The latter proceeded to indicate the qualities expected in a candidate for the degree of Bard, emphasizing that it would not be possible to admit anyone other than on the recommendation of a Bard who was present, or by examination of his skill in Poetic Compositions. The ceremony of admission, after suitable commendation and unanimous approval, was performed by the Officiating Bard, who held the sword with its point towards him while the entrant held the hilt, the former observing to the latter that, once admitted, he would be under an obligation not to show violence towards any man with the sword. After receiving him, the Officiating Bard tied a blue ribbon about his right arm. When all the Bards had been admitted, the sword was placed upon the stone at the centre of the circle.

While candidates were being admitted to the degree of Druid, the sword rested upon the stone at the centre of the circle and after due praise of the candidate had been received, and his qualifications recited, with no one dissenting, he was received by the Officiating Bard, who tied a white ribbon about his right arm ... The admission of others to the degree of Ovates was similarly carried out, except that these were adorned with green ribbons. After all the candidates had been admitted, the sword was taken up and all the bards touched its hilt as the Officiating Bard held the sheath into which the sword had been driven; and with this, the ceremony ended. The blue ribbon, worn by the *Bards,* is a symbol of truth; the white, innocence; the green, the arts.

Elizabeth Jones was admitted to the degree of Ovate by virtue of her literary merit. Verses in memory of the Rev. Peter Roberts and composed at the request of Thursday's president, were recited by the Rev. Gwallter Dafis, Mr Tomos Williams, John Cain Jones and Mr Robert Dafis; some of them were exceedingly good. Then Mr T. Williams and Mr R. Dafis sang verses to the harp in the old traditional Welsh manner. And, in response to earnest appeals, Mr Edward Jones, harpist to the Prince Regent, played his sweet-sounding harp in a most accomplished manner.

Thus came to an end the first ceremony of *Gorsedd Beirdd Ynys Prydain* to be held on Welsh soil.

The Carmarthen Eisteddfod was generally rated as a successful event, in addition to being an historic one, and was described by a contemporary writer as 'the mother of poets and of poetry in the present era'. But a discordant note came from the editor and founder of the first all-Welsh weekly, *Seren Gomer*, Joseph Harris (Gomer), a native of Wolfscastle in Pembrokeshire, who had been moved by the Puncheston revival of 1795 to become a Baptist minister. He complained about the worldly nature of the Carmarthen Eisteddfod: 'We have never heard a harp save while passing a beer-house and as to the atmosphere of dissipation and immorality of such places is inclined to cling to the instrument, it is not proper to stay and listen to it... We believe that harp-playing and playing the *crwth*, along with dancing, drunkenness, swearing, fighting and other evil practices, are things that Christians ought to avoid in all ways'.

In October of the same year a meeting of the Dyfed Society was held at the White Lion in Carmarthen, with Lord Dynevor in the chair. Bishop Burgess invited those present to meet on the following day at his palace at Abergwili, where a number of important decisions were taken including a resolve to catalogue unpublished Welsh manuscripts and to make a collection of all printed Welsh books. Iolo Morganwg was invited to take up residence at Carmarthen in order to supervise the publication of the manuscripts and advise upon them, but little was achieved.

The meeting agreed that efforts should be made to establish literary societies in the other kingdoms of Wales for the purpose of better promoting Welsh culture. At an inaugural meeting held, during the previous month, at Caernarfon under the chairmanship of Lord Bulkeley, the Gwynedd Cymmrodorion Society had been formed, and at a similar gathering held at Wrexham in October with Sir Watkin Williams Wynn presiding, the Powys Cymmrodorion Society was established. The Gwent Society was founded in 1821.

The Powys Society held its first eisteddfod at Wrexham in September 1820. Bardd Nantglyn won the chair for an ode in memory of King George III, and Ieuan Glan Geirionydd was awarded the prize for a *cywydd*.

The Gwynedd Society's first eisteddfod was held at Caernarfon in September 1821, under the presidency of the first Marquess of Anglesey. Prizes were offered for harp-playing and penillion singing, and the *awdl* and *cywydd* were limited to 200 lines so that the prize compositions could be recited in full by the successful poets. Those who had won prizes at the Carmarthen Eisteddfod of 1819, and at Wrexham in 1820, were barred from competing at Caernarfon. Among these was Bardd Nantglyn, chaired bard of the Powys Eisteddfod, who was given a hostile reception for his part in awarding the prize at the Denbigh eisteddfod in 1819 to Edward Hughes (Y Dryw), rector of Bodfari, instead of to the more deserving Dewi Wyn o Eifion (David Owen) for an *awdl* on *Elusengarwch* (Charity). The adjudication started a bitter controversy which raged for decades, and Dewi Wyn never competed at an eisteddfod again, but lines from his unsuccessful *awdl*, describing the plight of the impoverished worker, are among the best-known in the language:

> Aml y mae yn teimlo min
> Yr awel ar ei ewin; . . .
> Dwyn ei geiniog dan gwynaw,
> Rhoi angen un rhwng y naw.

(Often does he feel the edge of the breeze on his nails . . . Toiling in pain for his penny; sharing the needs of one among nine.)

The first session of the Caernarfon Eisteddfod began at noon on Tuesday, 12 September, at the County Hall, 'a low, mean-looking building, although it was neat and fairly commodious within'. The Marquess took the chair to the sound of a fanfare on the Corn Gwlad, the official Gorsedd horn, followed by Sir Watkin Williams Wynn's brass band playing 'See the Conquering Hero Comes'. He was supported on the platform by members of his family, the Earl and Countess of Uxbridge and the Ladies Georgina and Agnes Paget, and by the Bishop of Bangor and Mrs Majendie, Lord Newborough, Lord and Lady Selsey, Sir Charles

Morgan, M.P., Owen Williams, M.P., Sir Joseph Huddart, Sir Thomas Love Parry and other members of the local nobility. The Marquess apologised for his inability to deliver his address in Welsh but stressed that he was an ardent and patriotic Welshman. A translated summary of the speech was given by Dafydd Ddu Eryri, who also recited *englynion* which proved to be among the best ever composed. The chair was offered for an *awdl* on *Cerddoriaeth* (Music) and was won by Gwyndaf Eryri (Richard Jones: 1785-1848).

The nobility, led by the Marquess, ate fine dinners each evening at the Uxbridge Arms, now the Royal Hotel, but the bards fed on bowls of star-studded broth and quaffed quarts of home-brewed ale at the Goat Inn and other of the lowlier taverns in the town. On the Thursday night, they all assembled at the Harp Inn for a *noson lawen*.

As he opened the session on the second day, the Marquess observed that there were hundreds of people outside, unable to obtain admission to the already overcrowded hall. He opened the window and announced that they would all gather inside the castle walls, across the street from the County Hall. A crude platform was quickly erected but, after a while, rain began to fall and the meeting was adjourned until the following day.

The castle gates were thrown open again on the Thursday afternoon and the more adventurous among the spectators scaled the castle walls. High on the battlements 'stood an old goat with a long grey beard: for some hours he stood motionless on his perch, and to all seeming deeply interested in what was going on!' The afternoon was entirely taken up by a harp-playing competition: there were eleven competitors, four of whom were blind and a fifth, Jane Price, who formerly kept the Red Lion Inn at Caernarfon, was over ninety years of age!

An oratorio was performed at St. Mary's Church on the Thursday evening, and this was followed by a grand ball at the Guildhall, which was opened by Colonel Jones Parry and the Honourable Mrs Irby of Plas Llanidan. A contemporary chronicler recorded that this formed 'a very happy conclusion to the work of the Eisteddfod'.

The Gwent Society held its first eisteddfod at Brecon in 1822 under the presidency of Sir Charles Morgan, and from this time forth regional eisteddfodau were held fairly regularly.

At the Carmarthen Eisteddfod of 1823 the prizes were awarded to Daniel Ddu o Geredigion for his odes on *Coleg Dewi Sant* (St. David's College, Lampeter), the foundation stone of which had been laid by Bishop Burgess the previous year, and *Y Groegiaid a'r Tyrciaid* (the Turks had massacred 30,000 Greeks at Chios in 1822). A Gorsedd ceremony was held on the Saturday morning.

The Powys Society's Eisteddfod held at Welshpool in September 1824, under the presidency of Viscount Clive, provided the opportunity for Eben Fardd to write his famous *awdl, Dinistr Jeriwsalem* (Destruction of Jerusalem).

At an eisteddfod held at Llanfair Dyffryn Clwyd in 1827 the adjudicators in the *englyn* competition were Bardd Nantglyn and Robin Ddu Eryri (Robert Parry: 1804-92). They agreed on the best *englyn* but no one rose to claim the prize. Bardd Nantglyn said that he recognised the handwriting and volunteered to hand the prize of ten shillings to the winner. Later that year he published a book of verse under the title *Diliau Barddas* and in it appeared the winning *englyn!* Nantglyn had awarded the prize to himself, with the innocent connivance of Robin Ddu.

The 1828 Eisteddfod held at Denbigh under the auspices of the Gwynedd Society had, as its president, Sir Edward Lloyd, who later became the first Lord Mostyn, and representative of the family which had provided patronage for the Caerwys eisteddfodau three centuries earlier.

The Eisteddfod as we know it today grew out of the eisteddfodau promoted by the provincial literary societies, beginning with the Carmarthen Eisteddfod of 1819. Its promoters were followers of Iolo Morganwg, those for whom the idea of a druidic Gorsedd had a romantic appeal. The Carmarthen Eisteddfod became the pattern for the eisteddfodau of the future, with the Gorsedd as an essential part of it.

'Through the medium of the Gorsedd', wrote Professor G. J. Williams, 'and its symbol and doctrines and mythology, and the romantic consciousness of his writings, it may be said that Iolo began a new era. It was this consciousness, to a large extent, that explains the amazing growth of the Eisteddfod movement in the nineteenth century . . . Iolo gave to Wales a national institution . . . It is no exaggeration to say that the Eisteddfod belongs to him'.

The provincial eisteddfodau continued to flourish, even though they were not always well patronised by the public. Talhaiarn (John Jones: 1810-69), the poet and architect from Llanfair Talhaearn who supervised the building of the Crystal Palace, states that at an eisteddfod held in 1836 there were present 'llond berfa olwyn o bobl a llond gwagen o feirdd' (a barrow load of onlookers and a wagon load of bards). They were, however, rather lively affairs and frequently the centres of controversy.

The Eisteddfod held at Aberffraw in 1849 aroused considerable notoriety on account of the disagreement between the adjudicators, Eben Fardd, Iocyn Ddu (John Richards: 1795-1864) and Chwaneg Môn (Joseph Jones: 1787-1856). Eben Fardd was of the opinion that the prize for an *awdl* to *Y Greadigaeth* (The Creation) should be awarded to Emrys (William Amrose: 1813-73); Chwaneg Môn felt that it should go to Bardd Du Môn (Robert Williamson: 1807-52); Iocyn Ddu held that the ode submitted by Nicander (Morris Williams: 1809-74) deserved the chair, and he persuaded Chwaneg Môn to accept the same view. These two were not of the same calibre as Eben Fardd, either as poets or critics and, by all standards, the poem submitted by Emrys should have received the award. The prize of £25 and a medal went to Nicander, however, and the decision inspired a controversy which set Wales agog for the best part of a year. Newspapers and journals were lively with inflammatory letters between the leading Welsh poets and writers, and Emrys was persuaded to publish his poem, and to submit an official claim to the prize. It was pointed out that Iocyn Ddu and Chwaneg Môn were Anglicans and that Nicander was a curate at Amlwch at the time. Eben Fardd and Emrys, on the other hand, were Nonconformists. It may be that the Nonconformists felt that it was time to put an end to the ascendancy of the clergy in the promotion of eisteddfodau. It may also be that Eben Fardd suffered because his *Creation* was based on scientific and geological discovery rather than on the book of Genesis.

Gweirydd ap Rhys (Robert John Pryse), author of *Hanes y Brytaniaid a'r Cymry* (History of the Britons and the Welsh), *Hanes Llenyddiaeth Gymreig, 1300-1650* (History of Welsh Literature, 1300-1650) and of numerous other works, narrates how he attended the Aberffraw Eisteddfod expecting to be made a *pencerdd:* 'When I arrived at Aberffraw on 15th August 1849, the first day of the Eisteddfod, I told Clwydfardd, the Gorsedd Bard, that I had composed some shape of Awdl containing the Twenty-Four Measures, and that I wished to obtain consent to read it at the Gorsedd ceremony to be held on the third day in a bid to obtain the Order of Pencerdd! Clwydfardd laughed heartily and asked if I did not know that the Bardic Degrees had, for a long time, been Bard, Ovate and Druid ... He said that all that was now needed, in order to obtain one of the three degrees, was to get a Bard to propose the candidate. "But as for you," he said, "your work is sufficientiy known; on that account it will not be necessary for anyone to propose you." I hesitated after hearing this, (and I wanting to be a Pencerdd!) as to whether I should accept the important Order offered to me; but I was dragged away by two friends to the Gorsedd where I was solemnly exalted, by Dewi o Ddyfed and Clwydfardd, as a B.B.D., *Bardd Braint a Defod* (Bard by Privilege and Custom)!'

At the Rhuddlan Eisteddfod of 1850, the chief prize was awarded to Ieuan Glan Geirionydd for his poem *Yr Atgyfodiad* (The Resurrection). As far back as 1823 he had argued against a slavish attachment to *cynghanedd* and he and his fellow protagonists had reason to feel that they had achieved their object at Rhuddlan where, for the first time, bards were given the freedom to compose an ode either in free metre *(pryddest)* or in strict metre *(awdl)*. Ieuan Glan Geirionydd's poem in free metre was adjudged the best, and the second prize was awarded to Caledfryn, the chaired bard of the Beaumaris Eisteddfod of 1832, for his *awdl*. Ieuan's *pryddest* was a Miltonian poem of some three-thousand lines and one of the adjudicators pronounced that 'the whole poem is a body of divinity'. Eben Fardd had submitted a classical *pryddest* of about the same length in accordance with the fashion of the period. Such lengths were modest, however, when compared with Gwilym Hiraethog's *pryddest* to *Emmanuel* containing 22,000 lines.

The Eisteddfod took a new turn in 1858 when an attempt was made to reactivate the provincial eisteddfod of Powys (which still flourishes) and to end the disorderliness which had characterised recent events. In itself, it was probably the oddest eisteddfod ever to be held. It was organised by Ab Ithel (Rev. John Williams: 1811-62), a native of Llangynhafal in Denbighshire, a graduate of Jesus College, Oxford, who had been given the living of Llanymawddwy. In 1846, he and H. Longueville Jones initiated and edited *Archaeologica Cambrensis* and, a year later, they founded the Cambrian Archaeological Association, but they parted company when Ab Ithel became involved in the druidism of Iolo Morganwg. Ab Ithel then established the *Cambrian Journal*. He was regarded as one of the leading scholars of the day and was even considered for appointment to the chair of Celtic studies at Oxford, although this would appear to have been an over-estimate of his abilities. He was assisted in the organisation of the Llangollen Eisteddfod by his friends Môr Meirion (Rev. R. W. Morgan: 1815-99), born in Llangynfelin and curate of Tregynon in Montgomeryshire, and Carn Ingli (Joseph Hughes: 1803-63), a native of Newport in Pembrokeshire, who became curate of Meltham in Yorkshire and Secretary of the Association of Welsh Clergy in the West Riding.

The event was widely publicised and cheap trains were run to Llangollen for the benefit of members of the public who were to witness the most derisory scenes on an eisteddfod platform. Ab Ithel and his friends appeared in strange 'druidical' costumes, while Myfyr Morgannwg wore an egg on a string around his neck. Dr William Price of Llantrisant posed as 'archdruid' wearing a 'Davy Crockett' hat of fox fur and carrying a sword on his thigh, while his daughter appeared in her 'customary role' as *Iarlles Morgannwg* (Countess of Glamorgan).

The chair was awarded to Eben Fardd for his ode to *Maes Bosworth* (Bosworth Field) and Ceiriog won the prize for a poem to *Myfanwy Fychan*. Ab Ithel had suggested that a prize of a 'bardic tiara in gold' and £30 be offered for the best collection of works on 'the old druidic order'. The prize was awarded to him for material which he had copied from Iolo Morganwg's papers deposited at Llanofer, and which he had seen while gathering material for his *Cambrian Journal.* Several of the other prizes were awarded to members of Ab Ithel's family, and the substantial profits were pocketed by the three promoters. They refused to award a prize to Thomas Stephens for his *Madoc: An Essay on the Discovery of America by Madoc ap Owen Gwynedd in the Twelfth Century,* although it was far superior to the other entries, because he had suggested that the story might not be quite true!

Despite all this, the Great Eisteddfod of Llangollen, as it became known, was a notable landmark. Its very disorder and thievery confirmed the need for reform and led to discussion among men of letters on the desirability of having a central control. Glan Alun (Thomas Jones: 1811-66) and Creuddynfab (William Williams: 1814-69) were asked to prepare a report on the reorganisation of the festival.

The report was considered at the Denbigh Eisteddfod in 1860 and it was agreed that henceforth there should be a single great and National Eisteddfod held annually, alternatively in North and South Wales, both to include the adjoining parts of England where there were Welsh communities. An Eisteddfod Council of three hundred members was established for the purpose of organising the festival and to prepare subjects for the various competitions in good time so as to enable entrants to prepare work of a high standard. It also undertook the publication of the successful compositions, which it did in a quarterly journal called *Yr Eisteddfod,* edited by Creuddynfab from 1864 to 1866. Creuddynfab was appointed the first paid secretary of the Association.

The first Eisteddfod to follow the resolution made at Denbigh was the one held at Aberdare in 1861 which may, therefore, be regarded as the first National Eisteddfod. In his diary John Jones

(Eiddil Glan Cynon) refers to the Eisteddfod competition for a string of *englynion* to the 'United Eisteddfod of South and North Wales, the first of which is held at Aberdare in 1861'.

Though the pavilion in which the festival was to be held was wrecked by a storm, the Eisteddfod produced a memorable pastoral poem, for a prize of four guineas and a silver medal, in Ceiriog's *Alun Mabon*.

These new-style eisteddfodau also provided a non-sectarian, non-political platform which was soon seized by zealous reformers like Sir Hugh Owen and Henry Richard, 'The Apostle of Peace', and by well-meaning London Welshmen who were possessed by a ceaseless urge to reform. The Council was resolved to employ any means that would be 'likely to raise the social, moral and intellectual condition of the nation' and, in 1861 at the Aberdare Eisteddfod, Sir Hugh Owen, who was shortly to promote the idea of a University College of Wales at Aberystwyth, established 'the Social Science Section of the Eisteddfod'.

The Eisteddfod Council worked in close co-operation with the local committee in the organisation of the Caernarfon Eisteddfod of 1862. Hugh Owen played a vital role in obtaining the interest of Lord Penrhyn who had refused to take part in the festival: he paid him a visit at Penrhyn Castle and persuaded him to preside over one of the sessions and to make a contribution of £100.

The Eisteddfod was held within the walls of Caernarfon Castle, where seating had been provided for 4,500 people, under a canvas roof. A united service was held on the evening of Sunday, 24 August, and all the chapels in the town were closed so that their congregations could gather together in ecumenical worship.

On the Tuesday morning a procession formed at the Guildhall and moved to the Castle Square, where a Gorsedd ceremony was held. The ceremony was presided over by Gwalchmai (Richard Parry: 1803-97), who formally proclaimed the Eisteddfod.

The second day also opened with a Gorsedd ceremony, when several candidates submitted themselves to a rigid examination for degrees. The examiners were Clwydfardd (David Griffith: 1800-94), Gwalchmai, Nefydd (William Roberts: 1813-72), Ioan Emlyn (John Emlyn Jones: 1820-73) and Glan Alun. The successful candidates were initiated at a similar ceremony held the following morning.

Hwfa Môn (Rowland Williams: 1823-1905) was awarded the prize for an *awdl* to Y Flwyddyn (The Year) and was installed in the Chair in which Gwyndaf Eryri had been chaired in 1812. It was said that Eben Fardd was one of the eight other competitors and that his disappointment at his want of success was so great that it hastened his death.

The chairman of the Eisteddfod Council, the Rev. John Griffiths, rector of Neath and, later, Archdeacon of Llandaff, announced that a memorial had been received from Swansea asking that the National Eisteddfod should be held in that town in 1863, and that this had been favourably received. He confirmed that the National Eisteddfod would be held alternatively in north and south Wales in future, and that it had been formally put on record that 'the divisions and dissensions between the people of the North and of the South had been buried for ever'.

A Gorsedd ceremony was held at an early hour on the Friday morning on Castle Square, and the rest of the day was set aside for a conference on Social Science. Lord Penrhyn presided, and Sir Hugh Owen, who had long wanted to graft on to the Eisteddfod a meeting at which practical questions could be discussed, read a paper advocating night schools in Wales. Other papers included such topics as 'The employment of leisure hours by working men in Wales', 'Co-operative Societies', 'Club houses for the Working Classes', 'Life Assurance' and 'The advantages of instruction in the laws of health in common schools'.

It was during this Eisteddfod that Ceiriog (John Ceiriog Hughes:1832-87) suggested to Brinley Richards, that he should provide music for Ceiriog's poem *Ar Dywysog Gwlad y Bryniau,* later translated as 'God Bless the Prince of Wales', with a view to it becoming the national anthem of the Welsh people. The proposal was overtaken, however, by the appearance of *Hen Wlad Fy Nhadau* (Land of My Fathers), a poem by Evan James (1809-78), weaver and wool merchant of Pontypridd, set to music by his son, James James (1833-1902), although the air was later claimed to be an adaptation of *Tiptin o' Rosin the Beau,* from an old English comic opera. It was included in a collection of unpublished airs that was awarded the prize at the Llangollen Eisteddfod in 1858, and published by Owain Alaw in his *Gems of Welsh Melody* in 1860, following which it became popular and was sung regularly at Eisteddfodau and at Gorsedd ceremonies.

Fears that the Eisteddfod was in danger of becoming anglicised were expressed at the Chester Eisteddfod of 1866. The proclamation had been read in English by Talhaiarn who reminded the president of the day, Sir Watkin Williams Wynn, and the gathered assembly, that the wars between the Welsh and the English had long been over, 'never more to return; ... we are now to all intents and purposes, one people.' The President of the Council, the Rev.

John Griffiths, was unable to be present and, in his letter of apology for his absence, he expressed his own view on the place of the language: 'I am much attached to the old language and hope it will be long preserved, but I cannot sympathise with those amongst us who would exclude from profit or enjoyment everyone who cannot understand it.'

At this eisteddfod, according to an article in the *Manchester Guardian* of 3 September 1936, 'one of the hardest words in our language came unobtrusively into existence.' Matthew Arnold had been invited to be present but he could not attend and, anticipating the habits of Mr Bernard Shaw, wrote a letter instead: 'We in England have come to that point when the continued advance and greatness of our nation is threatened by one cause above all — far more than by the helplessness of an aristocracy whose day is fast coming to an end — far more than by the rawness of a lower class whose day is only just beginning — we are imperilled by what I call the Philistinism of our middle classes. On the side of beauty and taste, vulgarity; on the side of morals and feelings, coarseness; on the side of mind and spirit, unintelligence — this is Philistinism. What exactly the Chester Eisteddfod did may be forgotten, but *Philistinism* came to stay.' Arnold had adopted the term, not from the warlike Palestinian tribe, but from the German word *philister* applied by university students at Jena, in 1689, to 'outsiders' after a 'town and gown' row which resulted in a number of deaths and following which the university chaplain preached on the text: 'The Philistines be upon thee'.

The language theme recurred at the Carmarthen Eisteddfod in the following year when the Rev. Latimer Jones, vicar of St Peter's and president of the local committee, in his address at the opening session claimed that 'the Eisteddfod does not desire a separate national language, a separate nationality nor a separate and distinct existence' for Wales, and got a hostile reception from the audience. The local press, however, gave him credit for introducing 'what was much required — an English element — into the meetings, to an extent far greater than has ever been attempted,' and his sentiments were echoed by several other speakers including Judge John Johnes of Dolaucothi, Recorder of Carmarthen, who was murdered five years later by his own Irish butler. Controversy also arose over the engagement of professional singers from London 'to the exclusion of the Cambrian muse,' for which the composer Brinley Richards was largely held responsible.

Richards, the son of the organist of St Peter's, was a talented musician who became the director of the Royal Academy of Music and a pianist of national fame. In 1834, at the age of fifteen, he won a prize at the Morgannwg Eisteddfod for variations on the air *Llwyn Onn* (The Ash Grove), and over 250 of his compositions are listed in the British Museum catalogue of printed music.

The Carmarthen Eisteddfod of 1867 was described as 'a grand meeting of bards, literati and others interested in the prosperity of Wales and in its material and intellectual improvement,' which was regarded as a change from the time 'when wild looking men attired in night gowns met together to play harps and recite poetry.' A procession of some two thousand people formed on the Tuesday morning, led by the Mayor and Corporation, and marched through the banner-bedecked town. The Ivy Bush Hotel remembered the historic Eisteddfod of 1819 with a banner bearing the words *Home of the Bards : Old Ivy Bush*.

It was an eventful Eisteddfod in many respects. The weather was unkind: the roof of the £700 purpose-built pavilion was blown off as Madam Patey-Whitock sang *The Storm*. The manager of the London Zoological Gardens gave a late-night talk on snakes and serpents, and a reverend gentleman newly returned from Palestine advocated the establishment of a Welsh settlement in the Holy Land. Caledfryn (William Williams: 1801-69) and Cynddelw (Robert Ellis: 1812-75), adjudicators of the chair poem, failed to agree and Ceiriog was summoned as a referee. He awarded the chair to Gwalchmai. Llew Llwyfo, (Lewis William Lewis: 1831-1901), the idol of Welsh audiences, was described by Madam Patey-Whitock as 'a suitable specimen for a menagerie,' so little did she think of his singing. Brinley Richards felt obliged to resign as musical director of the Eisteddfod in view of the criticisms that had been levelled at him. The London papers lampooned the event and complained that too much place had been given 'to nationalistic speeches and diatribes against the Saxon press.' But it is memorable for the introduction of new ideas, including the extension of activities to include lectures and exhibitions of archaeological, geological, botanical, entomological and industrial interest. And it was the first occasion for a crown to be awarded for the best poem in ordinary verse *(pryddest)*. It was won by Hwfa Môn, who had been awarded the Chair at Caernarfon in 1862.

The 1868 Eisteddfod was held at Ruthin from Tuesday to Friday, 4-7 August, in a pavilion made of timber and designed to hold 5,000 people. The Chair was offered for the best *awdl* not exceeding 1,000 lines on *Eleias y Thesbiad* (Elijah the Tishbite) along with a cash prize of £20. There were seven competitors but the adjudicator, Gwilym Hiraethog, was unable to declare one of them worthy of the Chair. 'The elongated faces of the bards were a sight to see,' and one of the disappointed competitors, Llew Llwyfo, stormed against the decision, while Tudno (Thomas Tudno Jones : 1844-95) 'emitted an englyn which spoke of the coveted chair as so much timber for sale.' The Crown was awarded to Talhaiarn for the best *pryddest* on *Ruthin Castle*.

A staggering prize of 150 guineas, albeit for a difficult task, was offered for the best essay (in English, Welsh, French or German) on *The Origins of the English Nation, with reference more especially to the question, How they are descended from the Ancient Britons?* The adjudicator was Lord Strangford, the linguist and philologist, who awarded the handsome prize to Dr John Beddoe, M.D., LL.D., F.R.S., Vice-President of the Clifton Anthropological Society, Bristol.

The Ruthin Eisteddfod proved a financial liability because the local committee would not hand over the proceeds to the Council, and some of the members of the Council had to make good the loss out of their own pockets. The Eisteddfod Council came to an untimely end after only seven years of activity and, for the next twelve years, several proposals were made to establish a new central organisation.

At the Portmadoc Eisteddfod of 1872, proposals were put forward for the establishment of a Welsh Antiquarian Society. This was one of a number of efforts made to provide a central Welsh cultural organisation, the need for which was felt more keenly as the demands for improved education increased. Over three hundred applications for membership of the Society had been received by the Mold Eisteddfod of 1873, where Y Thesbiad: (John Roose Elias: 1819-81) the promoter of the idea, formally proposed its formation, along with the publication of an antiquarian journal.

On the following day, however, a suggestion was made by Ceiriog that a Society be formed of recognised Welsh poets, writers and musicians, to be known as *Urdd y Ford Gron* (The Order of the Round Table). Its aims would be to reform the management of the Eisteddfod and, in an unobtrusive way, to 'diminish the disorder and confusion of the Eisteddfodau and utilise the great power which the national gathering possessed.' This suggestion was followed by a proposal to revive the Honourable Society of Cymmrodorion, which had become dormant in 1787 and, after revival, again in 1843. Y Gohebydd (John Griffiths: 1821-77) supported this proposal and suggested that the Musical Prize Fund Committee, which had raised funds to meet the expenses of the

61

South Wales Choral Union's visit to London when competing for the £1000 prize trophy offered by the Director of the Crystal Palace, should be 'the nucleus of a Society for the encouragement of literature and fine arts in Wales.' This was generally accepted by all interested parties at the Mold Eisteddfod, and the third Cymmrodorion Society was formally established in London in the following November.

The next eisteddfod of any note was the Wrexham Eisteddfod of 1876. The prize for the best *awdl* had been awarded to Taliesin o Eifion (Thomas Jones : 1820-76), inn-sign painter of Llangollen, but when it was learnt that he had died, the Chair was ceremonially draped in black as the audience stood in silence.

Clwydfardd claimed that he was 'licensed as Archdruid of the Gorsedd of the Bards of the Isle of Britain' at the Wrexham Eisteddfod, but maintained that he had already been appointed to that office in 1860.

The Caernarfon Eisteddfod of 1877 was proclaimed at a Gorsedd ceremony held in a field near Twthill, on 18 September 1876, and a bond was delivered by 201 inhabitants of the town at a public meeting that evening, providing a guarantee of £10 each against any loss that might be incurred in staging the festival.

The Eisteddfod was opened at nine o'clock on Tuesday, 21 August 1877, with a Gorsedd ceremony conducted by Clwydfardd on the green sward within the walls of Caernarfon Castle, close to Queen Eleanor's Gate.

The proceedings at the Pavilion, a permanent building specially erected for the occasion in a field behind Bangor Street, were opened by the Mayor of Caernarfon, Councillor Hugh Pugh. Lord Penrhyn, presiding on Wednesday, reminded his audience that he had also presided over the same session in 1862 and repeated his 'warning' that standards were low, and added: 'When I witness the appreciation of talent such as we have brought together on this occasion, I can only wonder that mediocrity is so often unduly exalted, and a quick, clever people degraded by parading tenth-rate talent as though it were our country's best.'

The great audience of 8,000 was so impressed by a speech delivered by Henry Richard, M.P., 'the Apostle of Peace', that a resolution was enthusiastically adopted petitioning Parliament to grant-aid the new University College of Aberystwyth.

The chair was awarded to Gwilym Eryri (William Roberts : 1844-95), of Portmadoc, for his *awdl* on *Ieuenctid* (Youth), and a special prize was offered for a poem on *Cadair Ddu Wrecsam* (The Black Chair of Wrexham) in memory of Taliesin o Eifion.

Among those admitted to the Gorsedd on the Friday morning was the celebrated Adelina Patti, who chose to be known in bardic circles as 'Eos Prydain' (Nightingale of Britain).

The Eisteddfod returned to Caernarfon sooner than expected owing to the failure of Holywell to accept the festival in 1880. A Proclamation Ceremony had been arranged to be held inside the castle walls on the morning of 24 October 1879, but the skies opened and the bards met at high noon on Castle Square for a brief ceremony before retiring for luncheon at the Sportsman Hotel.

In April 1880, Sir Hugh Owen read a paper on Eisteddfod reform to the Honourable Society of Cymmrodorion at the Freemasons' Tavern, Great Queen Street, London. In it, he expressed his belief that 'the present plan of devolving upon a local committee the whole of the care and responsibilities connected with the holding of a National Eisteddfod is, in many respects, unsatisfactory,' and suggested that it was 'desirable that a permanent Association be formed, and an Executive Council appointed, for the purpose — among others — of co-ordinating with the local committee and assisting in rendering the Eisteddfod arrangements in all their parts such as may still further increase the popularity and extend the usefulness of our national institution. The proposed Association to be designated *The National Eisteddfod Association,* and to be composed of subscribers and honorary members . . . and to have a President, Vice-Presidents and an Executive Council. The Council to be designated *The National Eisteddfod Council* and to be composed of representatives from all parts of the Principality, selected with special reference to their fitness for the position. The Council to appoint a Chairman, Treasurer, and Secretary. The Association to hold an Annual Meeting when the Council shall submit a report of their proceedings together with a statement of their accounts, and when the Council will be re-elected.'

He went on to indicate some of the matters which would engage the attention of the new Council. These included the raising, by means of annual subscriptions and donations, of an Eisteddfod Fund that would enable the Council to offer prizes for competitions and in other ways to promote the usefulness of the Eisteddfod. He believed that contributions to the extent of at least £1,000 a year could be obtained towards this Fund. The Council should secure the holding of one National Eisteddfod in each year, and decide its venue in North Wales and South Wales alternately. It would assist in providing a suitable pavilion in which the Eisteddfod could be held, where other suitable accommodation did not exist, and he contended that it might be practicable to provide a mobile pavilion for this purpose thereby reducing the expenditure which had usually attended the erection of a pavilion. The Council would assist in selecting appropriate subjects for the competitions and in determining the sums to be awarded as prizes. It would endeavour to widen the range of subjects for competition by embracing works of art and handicrafts. It would discourage the acceptance of prizes offered by individuals to which any conditions were attached. It would secure men of eminence to preside at the eisteddfod meetings and select well-qualified persons to act as adjudicators. It would assist in the preparation of a programme and would uphold the authority of the Gorsedd with its mystic rites and its ceremonies. The Council would publish a volume of the transactions of each eisteddfod, a copy of which would be presented to generous subscribers. It would 'be the endeavour of the Council to assist in making the Eisteddfod the upholder of public virtue, as well as the promoter of excellency in literature, poetry, music, art, manufacture and handicraft, and to assist in excluding from the Eisteddfod proceedings whatever may be deemed low, vulgar or in bad taste; as this highest court of the nation ought to be characterized in all its aspects by propriety, decorum, and even dignity, while its decisions ought to be marked by soundness of judgement and the strictest impartiality.'

The proposals were warmly commended by the chairman of the meeting, Professor (later Sir) John Rhys, of Jesus College, Oxford, and by several of the members of the Society, including Prince Louis Lucien Bonaparte, and it was unanimously resolved that the Honourable Society should take steps to secure the formation of a permanent organisation to assist in the conduct of the National Eisteddfod.

Sir Hugh Owen read his paper again during the Caernarfon Eisteddfod, at a meeting of the Cymmrodorion Society held in the Magistrates' Room at the Caernarfon Town Hall on 25 August 1880 and, on the following morning, a paper was read on the same subject by Mrs Anne Thomas, wife of the vicar of Llandegai, in which she advocated the incorporation of the Eisteddfod under a Royal Charter and its endowment by the Government. The matter was discussed at considerable length at a further meeting held that evening under the chairmanship of J. H. Puleston, M.P., but a motion that the Cymmrodorion Society should be authorised to carry out the proposals in the papers was opposed, on the grounds that control would go to London. A compromise was then reached by appointing a Provisional Committee in conjunction with the Society, the majority of the members being drawn from the

Gorsedd of Bards, and the following resolutions were made:

(i) that a *National Eisteddfod Association* be forthwith established;

(ii) that the following gentlemen (with power to add to their number) be invited to act, in conjunction with the Cymmrodorion Society, as a Provisional Committee which shall consider and define the scope and functions of the Association:

Clwydfardd, Dewi Wyn, Hwfa Môn, Ceiriog, Gwalchmai, Ioan Arfon, Llew Llwyfo, Dafydd Morgannwg, Glanmor, Iolo Trefaldwyn, Gwilym Alltwen, Nathan Dyfed, Owain Alaw, Myfyr, Cynfaen, Alaw Ddu, David Jenkins, Emlyn Evans, Eos Morlais, Idris Fychan, Glan Menai, B. G. Evans, C. Wilkins, E. T. Davies, Owen Parry, W. Frimston, D. C. Davies;

(iii) that the Provisional Committee shall meet at .ie Raven Hotel, Shrewsbury, at 10 a.m., on Friday, the 17th September, 1880;

(iv) that Mr T. Marchant Williams, B.A., be requested to act as Honorary Secretary.

Sir Watkin Williams Wynn was elected President of the Association and he remained in that office until 1884, and Sir Lewis Morris was appointed Chairman of the Council that succeeded the Provisional Committee.

Penydarren Park, Merthyr Tydfil, was the venue of the 1881 Eisteddfod. Watcyn Wyn won the Crown for a poem on *Bywyd* (Life), and the Chair for an *awdl* on *Cariad* (Love) was awarded to Dyfed (Evan Rees : 1850-1923) who also won a prize of two guineas for a satirical poem on *Erlidwyr yr Eisteddfod* (The Persecutors of the Eisteddfod). A prize of ten guineas, and a gold medal, was offered for an epic poem to the Duke of Wellington.

The first Annual Meeting of the National Eisteddfod Association was held at the Castle Hotel, Merthyr, during the Eisteddfod, with the Archdruid Clwydfardd presiding.

The 1883 Eisteddfod at Cardiff was opened shortly after ten o'clock on the morning of Monday, 6 August, at a ceremony conducted by 'the venerable bard Clwydfardd' within the Gorsedd Circle erected in a field adjoining the Taff Vale Railway Company's engine shed. A commentator remarked that it was regrettable that the Gorsedd, 'one of the few links which bind the Eisteddfod, as we know it, to a remote and honoured past' should have been held 'amid such incongruous surroundings,' and complained that 'the charm of an ancient and impressive rite was destroyed by the screeching of railway locomotives on the one side and by the many hideous noises of a show-ground on the other.'

The Marquess of Bute presided over the morning meeting of the Eisteddfod and delivered an address on 'The Ethnology of the Welsh' which was later published in the Transactions of the Cymmrodorion. The prize of £100 for an essay on 'The History of Welsh Literature from the year 1300 to the year 1650' was won by Gweirydd ap Rhys (R. J. Pryse : 1807-99). Dewi Wyn o Esyllt (Thomas Essile Davies : 1820-91) received an award of twenty guineas for the best *awdl* in memory of Sir Hugh Owen, but no one was deemed worthy of the prize for an essay on Sir Hugh's 'Life and Labours'.

The Chair was offered for an *awdl* on *Y Llong* (The Ship), together with a prize of twenty guineas and a gold medal. Only three entries were received but none was worthy of the prize.

The streets of Cardiff were decorated with Venetian masts, decked with shields, and festoons of banners, with a huge triumphal arch over the entrance to the Eisteddfod field. The Mayor (Mr G. A. Stone) gave a banquet in the Town Hall in honour of the occasion.

Six choirs had entered for the chief choral competition, which was won by the Penrhyn Quarries Choir. The 'elongated parallelogram of a building' was packed with spectators eager to hear the choirs and unwilling to give a hearing to the president of the day, the Dean of Llandaff, despite his declaration that 'only treachery and cowardice would counsel Wales to fling away the speech which is her *differentia* among the nations.'

The third annual meeting of the National Eisteddfod Association was held at the Angel Hotel, Cardiff, with Sir Lewis Morris in the chair. A petition from the leading townspeople of Liverpool inviting the 1884 Eisteddfod, was presented by Llyfrbryf (Isaac Foulkes : 1836-1904) and Llew Wynne, Secretary of the Liverpool Welsh Choral Union. The petition was granted, but the Liverpool Committee was urged to curtail presidential speeches to twenty minutes each, and to see that the remarks of the adjudicators 'should be made as short as is compatible with full and efficient adjudications.'

The Cymmrodorion Section of the National Eisteddfod Association met on the Saturday evening prior to the opening of the Eisteddfod to hear an address by Sir Lewis Morris on the state of education in Wales. Other evenings were devoted to the Education,

Art and Science Sections of the Cymmrodorion. Under the auspices of the Art Section, James Milo Griffiths, the sculptor who had been awarded the art prize, delivered an address on 'The Eisteddfod in its relation to Art'. Having traced iconic art to the book of Genesis, where Rachel quits her father's dwelling taking with her certain images, he deplored the absence of Welsh art and urged the Eisteddfod Association to take a lead in its promotion. A move in this direction had already been made at Cardiff with the staging of an exhibition and with the founding of the Art Section, the inspiration for which had come from the Cardiff artist and naturalist Arlunydd Pen-y-garn (T. H. Thomas : 1839-1915).

The 1884 Eisteddfod was proclaimed on Kensington Fields, Liverpool, on 10 November 1883, by the Archdruid Clwydfardd.

The Eisteddfod was held in a large pavilion, specially erected within The Haymarket in Cazneau Street, and decorated with flags, and with heraldic devices around its walls. Retiring rooms were provided, and cloakrooms, refreshment rooms and a room with post and telegraph facilities.

At the opening Gorsedd ceremony held on Austin Hill, the bards wore sashes and aprons of blue silk bearing the secret symbols of *Gorsedd Beirdd Ynys Prydain*.

Despite the vastness of the pavilion, thousands of spectators had to be turned away, and there were murmurs about 'the mammoth character of the Eisteddfod'.

The Archdruid Clwydfardd was assisted in the chairing ceremony by Hwfa Môn and by Gwilym Alltwen, 'the Knight-Master of the Ceremonies' and the Sword Bearer, Ceiriog. The Chair was presented by the Cymmrodorion Society for the best *awdl* to commemorate Gwilym Hiraethog and was awarded to Dyfed who was chaired 'according to the Ancient Rites of the Bards of the Isle of Britain'. Madam Edith Wynne (Eos Cymru) emerged from her retirement to sing, as the chairing song, 'Far greater in his lowly state' from Gounod's *La Reine de Saba*.

Major W. Cornwallis West, the Lord Lieutenant of Denbigh-shire, deplored the standards in art and urged that promising students be sent to Mr Hubert Herkomer's school in London.

The 1885 Eisteddfod was conducted in a spacious pavilion erected for the occasion at Aberdare and it opened with a Gorsedd ceremony held on the Tuesday morning, 25 August, in a grassy enclosure close to the pavilion.

The first session of the Eisteddfod was held in the pavilion at eleven o'clock on the same morning, with Sir George Elliott, M.P., presiding, supported on the platform by Lord Aberdare, Matthew

67

Arnold, Clwydfardd, Hwfa Môn, Dyfed, Llew Llwyfo, Arlunydd Pen-y-garn, Pencerdd Gwalia, Caradog and others. The competitions during the first day included the harp solo, contralto solo, an englyn on 'Electricity', an essay on 'Welsh Social Life' and the Brass Band competition. Sir George entertained members of the Eisteddfod Association to luncheon served in a marquee on the lawn of Aberaman House.

The President for Wednesday was Mr J. C. Parkinson, D.C.L., and among those supporting him on the platform were Professor John Rhys, Professor Henry Reichel and Principal Viriamu Jones. The competitions included a pedal harp solo, oil painting, an original collection of folklore of Glamorgan, which was won by Cadrawd (Thomas Christopher Evans: 1846-1918) of Llangynwyd, an essay on 'The Importance and Benefit of Utilizing Leisure Hours', letter-cutting in stone, as well as choral competitions. These were followed by the chairing ceremony, when a carved oak Chair was offered for the best *awdl*, not to exceed one thousand lines, on *Y Gwir yn erbyn y Byd* (The Truth against the World). The bards assembled upon the stage and after the adjudication had been delivered by Hwfa Mon, he and Dyfed proceeded through the large audience to lead the successful poet, Watcyn Wyn, of Ammanford, to the platform. The successful bard was greeted with *See the Conquering Hero Comes* sung by Hywel Cynon, and with congratulatory verses by numerous bards.

Lord Aberdare presided over Thursday's proceedings and the audience was estimated at between six and seven thousand. Dr Matthew Arnold was introduced to the audience as one of the most devoted students of the Celtic character and literature. In his address he admitted that he had been interested in the Eisteddfod for the last twenty years but the sight of the immense audience had exceeded anything that he supposed possible. He had a poor hearing, however, and sat down before completing his speech.

Owing to the inclement weather the Gorsedd ceremony had to be postponed until the afternoon, when Watcyn Wyn, D. Onllwyn Brace and Jonathan Rees (Nathan Wyn) were initiated as bards.

Colonel Kemeys-Tynte of Cefn Mabli presided over Friday's competitions which included a translation of Euripides's *Alcestis*, for which a prize of £50 had been offered by the Marquess of Bute.

The Annual Meeting of the National Eisteddfod Association was held at the Queen's Hotel, Aberdare. Owing to the death of the president, Sir Watkin Williams Wynn, the Archdruid Clwydfardd presided and announced that the Marquess of Bute had accepted the presidency.

A petition was presented 'to the Bards, Ovates and Druids of the Isle of Britain in Gorsedd assembled at Aberdare, and to the National Eisteddfod Association' inviting the Eisteddfod to London in the following terms:

Fellow Countrymen. We, the undersigned, being Welshmen residing in London beg to apply to you for permission to hold the National Eisteddfod of Wales for 1887 in London. The following are the considerations which induce us to make this application, viz.,

(i)   that in accordance with the custom generally acknowledged of late, and in pursuance of an understanding arrived at when the National Eisteddfod Association was established, the National Eisteddfod of Wales shall be held alternately in North and South Wales.

(ii) that as the National Eisteddfod of Wales for 1886 is to be held in Caernarvon, that the 1887 should be held in South Wales.

(iii) that according to ancient and recognized Bardic Statutes, London forms part of Gwent and Morgannwg, and is mentioned as one of the places in which the Eisteddfod and Chair of that province may fitly be held and honoured.

(iv) that the National Eisteddfod of Wales was held very successfully in Liverpool in 1885, a precedent has been created for holding the Eisteddfod outside the Principality.

(v)   that if the National Eisteddfod of Wales be held in London in 1887 we have every reason to believe that it will be attended with great success.

Upon the strength of the statements made above, we ask that it may be proclaimed at Aberdare that the Eisteddfod of 1887 shall be held in London; and, therefore, that a Deputation nominated by us may be heard in support of the request of this petition.

We also pledge ourselves that if our request be granted, no effort of ours shall be wanting to make the Eisteddfod of 1887 worthy of its predecessors, and that it shall be planned and carried out as a Welsh gathering; that it shall be as Welsh as possible in every particular, and we will withstand all suggestions that may tend to give it an English character and complexion.

The petition was signed by thirty gentlemen, including David

Evans, Alderman and Sheriff of the City of London, Lewis Morris, Isambard Owen, T. Marchant Williams, John Thomas (harpist to the Queen), J. Milo Griffith and E. Vincent Evans, Joint-Secretary of the National Eisteddfod Association with W. E. Davies, who presented the petition.

An application was also read on behalf of the inhabitants of Aberystwyth, appealing for the Eisteddfod to be held in that town, but the Annual Meeting recommended to 'the Bards in Gorsedd' that the 1887 Eisteddfod should be held in London. The decision lay with the Gorsedd. Gwalchmai had reminded the assembly at Liverpool the previous year that 'it must not be forgotten that the Gorsedd was the governing Eisteddfodic power, and that in the Gorsedd Circle alone was vested supreme authority.'

The 1886 Eisteddfod at Caernarfon was held in the pavilion which had been erected for the festival of 1867. The platform was decorated with colourful banners provided by Sir Love Jones-Parry of Madryn, and the walls were hung with the names of former patrons and poets and musicians. The town was gay with flags and bunting.

A Gorsedd ceremony held in the grounds of Caernarfon Castle on the Wednesday morning was attended by the Lord Mayor of London (the Right Hon. Alderman J. Staples). He, accompanied by the Mayor (Alderman Lewis Lewis) and Corporation of Caernarfon, arrived in a procession led by the band of the 4th Bn. Royal Welch Fusiliers. The Archdruid Clwydfardd installed the Lord Mayor an ovate in the Gorsedd of Bards, by the bardic name of 'Gwyddon'. Gwyddon was the chief justice of Britain in Celtic times, and as the Lord Mayor of London was the first magistrate in the land, the pseudonym was considered appropriate. The Lord Mayor, in thanking the Bards for the honour bestowed upon him, said he had been brought up in that unique area of druidical remains — Stonehenge! Later, from the Eisteddfod platform, he stated that he was present as the representative of the citizens of London, so many of whom were Welshmen, to extend a welcome to the National Eisteddfod to be held in the metropolis the following year. He was presented with a bolt of Welsh homespun and, in the evening, was entertained at a banquet by the Mayor and Corporation at the Sportsman Hotel.

The chairing ceremony took place on the Thursday afternoon. The stage conductor, Llew Llwyfo, invited the Archdruid and the bards to take their place on the stage, where they formed a semi-circle. Gwalchmai delivered the adjudication and said that he and his fellow-adjudicators, Elis Wyn o Wyrfai, (Canon Ellis

Roberts : 1827-95) and Gwilym Eryri, were unanimous in awarding the Chair, and the prize of £20, to Tafolog (Richard Davies : 1830-1904) for his *awdl* on the subject *Gobaith* (Hope). The successful poet stood up in the midst of the vast audience until the Archdruid and Hwfa Môn came to bring him to the platform, where he was greeted with a fanfare of trumpets. As he stood before the oak chair, the Archdruid drew the Sword from its sheath and called 'A oes heddwch?' (Is there peace?) three times. The audience replied 'Heddwch' each time : the Sword was returned to its sheath and the Chaired Bard sat in his Chair to tumultuous acclamation.

The town of Wrexham was gaily decorated to welcome the Eisteddfod in September 1888 and a suitable pavilion was erected in Grove Park to seat 7,000 spectators. At the Gorsedd ceremony held in a stone circle surrounded by a blue rope on an open space in Argyle Street, Clwydfardd admitted Sir Watkin Williams Wynn an ovate under the title of 'Eryr Eryrod Eryri' and Professor (later Sir) John Rhys was invested with the name 'Rhys Blaen Rheidol'. The Rev. H. Elvet Lewis of Hull, who was admitted under the name of 'Elfed', won the prize for the best *pryddest* to *Y Sabbath yng Nghymru* (The Sabbath in Wales). More important, he received the award for the best *rhieingerdd* (love poem) to *Llyn y Morynion* (The Lake of the Maidens), in which he introduced a new metre and form based on a Breton model. The chair for the *awdl* to *Peroriaeth* (Melody) was awarded to Tudno, who had previously won the Chairs at Pwllheli in 1875 and Caernarfon in 1877. Charles Ashton, a policeman at Dinas Mawddwy and self-taught literary historian, was awarded the prize of £20 for an essay on *Gorsedd Beirdd Ynys Prydain,* which was published in the *Transactions of the National Eisteddfod of Wales* for that year.

In 1889, the National Eisteddfod was held 'in a grand pavilion erected at Cerrigcochion, Brecon, by Mr Clark, of Stoke-on-Trent, and designed to accommodate about 8,000 people.' It was opened with a Gorsedd ceremony in a circle within the ruins of Brecon Castle, where it had been proclaimed the previous year as indicated by an inscription, in gilt letters, on the Logan Stone : 'Maen Gorsedd Beirdd Ynys Prydain. Aberhonddu, Gorph. 10, 1888' (The Gorsedd Stone of Bards of the Isle of Britain. Brecon, July 10, 1888).

A report in the *Cardiff Times* stated that a special feature of the opening session of the Eisteddfod was a speech by Father Ignatius of Llanthony Abbey, who 'commenced a vigorous and impassioned address by exclaiming at the top of his voice, in pure Welsh : "Os anghofiaf di, Jerusalem, anghofied fy neheulaw ganu" (If I forget thee, O Jerusalem, let my right hand forget her cunning), — a sentiment which elicited hearty applause'.

The highlight of the Brecon Eisteddfod, however, was the visit of Madam Adelina Patti on the Wednesday afternoon : 'At one o'clock the vast pavilion was literally crammed and it was estimated that at least 12,000 persons had assembled to hear the famous Queen of Song. As the minutes passed the excitement became intense, and it was utterly impossible to proceed with the adjudications. Mabon, with characteristic tact, came into the breach and started *Hen Wlad fy Nhadau* ... Even this did not fill the gap and after the conductor had announced that the train bearing Madam Patti had arrived, the interval was spent in singing *O fryniau Caersalem.* In the meantime the band of the 1st South Wales Borderers was despatched to the station to accord the Queen songstress a musical welcome. Thousands of people who were unable to obtain admission to the pavilion lined the route and Madam Patti was vociferously cheered as she drove along. When the strains of the band were heard at the pavilion, the vast sea of humanity relapsed into silence and every eye was turned upon the platform entrance', and, as she ascended the platform, 'such a cheer of welcome broke forth from the throats of the assembled thousands as perhaps has never before been heard among the beloved hills and valleys of Wales'. The great soprano responded by singing an aria from *La Somnambula, The Last Rose of Summer* and *Home Sweet Home,* 'but the greatest impression on the audience was made, undoubtedly, in her rendering of the Welsh National Song *Hen Wlad fy Nhadau,* to which the entire audience, led by Mabon, contributed a chorus.'

Mabon (William Abraham : 1842-1922), apart from being the first president of the South Wales Miners' Federation and Member of Parliament for the Rhondda division, was well known as a conductor of eisteddfodau and, with his powerful tenor voice, he often sang to the vast audiences.

The Cymmrodorion Section heard papers on 'Welsh Spelling Reform' by Professor (later Sir) John Morris-Jones and Professor (later Sir) J. E. Lloyd, and gave serious thought to the publication of Welsh historical records.

A formal constitution for the National Eisteddfod Association was formulated at the Brecon Eisteddfod and this was accepted at the Bangor Eisteddfod the following year. It laid down the relationship between the Association and the Gorsedd and it was agreed that members of the Gorsedd should also be members of the National Eisteddfod Association.

The Bangor Eisteddfod opened on 2 September 1890, with a

Gorsedd ceremony held in a field near the railway station following which a procession moved to the pavilion which had been erected in Ffordd y Garth. Viscount Cranbrook, Lord President of the Council, presided over the proceedings of the day.

At the Gorsedd ceremony on the Thursday morning it was announced that Sir John Puleston, M.P. and Treasurer of the National Eisteddfod Association, and Mr G. W. Taylor, of the Colonial Institute, intended presenting the Archdruid with a robe worthy of his high office. The Grand Sword had already been presented by Philip Yorke of Erddig, and a *Corn Gwlad* by the Mayor of Pwllheli.

Queen Marie of Roumania was present at the ceremony and was admitted to the Gorsedd of Bards under the bardic name 'Carmen Sylva'. The following day she read a poem from the Eisteddfod platform in praise of Wales and of the bards.

The 1892 Eisteddfod was opened on 6 September, at Rhyl, with a Gorsedd ceremony held in the grounds of the Palace and Summer Gardens. A pavilion of palatial proportions, with a dome-like roof and capable of seating 10,000 people, had been built for the occasion.

The Lord Mayor of London (Sir David Evans, K.C.M.G.) presided on the morning of the first day and, at a special ceremony at noon, he was invested with the degree of Ovate of the Gorsedd of Bards.

On Thursday, 'the great chair day of the Eisteddfod', the adjudicators, Watcyn Wyn and Gwynedd (Thomas Edwards : 1844-1924) could not agree on the award of the Chair for an *awdl* to *Y Cenhadwr* (The Missionary) and Hwfa Môn was asked to act as referee. He, rather unenthusiastically, awarded the Chair to Gurnos Jones, of Porthcawl.

The Gorsedd ceremony which opened the Caernarfon Eisteddfod on the morning of Tuesday, 10 July 1894, was held in the Castle Square. It was a colourful and historical occasion because 'for the first time within recent memory, the druids, bards, and ovates were distinguished by coloured robes according to their orders, with which the members of the Gorsedd had been supplied through the generosity of Lord Bute, Lord Mostyn, Mr Watkin Williams Wynn, and other subscribers.'

In his presidential address at the opening session, Sir Lewis Morris, Chairman of the Eisteddfod Council, stated that 'the Eisteddfod was no longer the sole instrument of education — the only University of the Welsh people. There was another University (of Wales) established this very year by the grant of a Royal

Charter.' He felt that the visit of the Prince of Wales to Caernarfon the following day was also a historic occasion that gave recognition to the National Eisteddfod, for 'after all these years of opposition, of ridicule, of depreciation, at last the old Welsh institution was placed under the patronage of its Prince.'

The Prince and Princess and their daughters, the Princesses Victoria and Maud, arrived at the thronged Pavilion to the strains of a consort of harps conducted by Pencerdd Gwalia, harpist to the Queen. They received bardic addresses from Elis Wyn o Wyrfai, Dyfed and Watcyn Wyn, and a formal address from the people of Wales read in Welsh by the Mayor of Caernarfon (Councillor J. Issard Davies) and in English by Lord Penrhyn. The Prince, in responding, apologised for his inability to do so in Welsh for, in that respect, his education had been greatly neglected!

The Rev. Ben Davies, Pant-teg was crowned by Hwfa Môn for his *pryddest* to *Tennyson* during a ceremony held on the Pavilion platform, and invested by the Princess of Wales. The royal party then proceeded to Castle Square to attend a Gorsedd ceremony. The Prince of Wales was conducted to the foot of the Logan Stone, where the Archdruid Clwydfardd tied a green ribbon round his arm and admitted him to the Gorsedd as an Honorary Ovate under the title of 'Iorwerth Dywysog'. The Princess was likewise initiated as 'Hoffedd Prydain', Princess Victoria as 'Buddug' and Princess Maud as 'Mallt'.

The adjudicators could not agree on the award of the Chair for an *awdl* on *Hunan-aberth* (Self-sacrifice) but Dyfed and Pedrog, with Tudno dissenting, declared Elfed worthy of the Eisteddfod's chief prize, and he was duly chaired by Clwydfardd, who performed the ceremony for the last time.

The Llanelli Eisteddfod had been proclaimed in the People's Park, Llanelli, in June 1894, with a *Gorsedd Gyfarch* (Gorsedd of Salutation) being held in the morning, and a *Gorsedd Hawl* (Gorsedd of Legal Right) in the afternoon. The Eisteddfod was opened on the morning of Tuesday, 30 July 1895 with a Gorsedd ceremony at which Watcyn Wyn announced from the Logan Stone that Hwfa Môn had been appointed Archdruid in succession to Clwydfardd, who had died the previous October. Arlunydd Pen-y-garn was appointed Herald Bard.

That the matter of housing the festival was already a problem is indicated by the offer of a prize of £25, at Llanelli, for 'a design for a moveable permanent pavilion, suited to the requirements of the National Eisteddfod, with complete specifications, estimates and full details,' but only one set of plans came to hand, with a design that appeared to be a facsimile of the pavilion erected at Pontypridd in 1893.

In his presidential address at the opening session at the Pavilion, Sir Arthur Stepney reminded his audience that this was the first time for the National Eisteddfod to be held at Llanelli. Sir John Jones-Jenkins, M.P., the afternoon's president, announced that 'the Scotch Highlanders had got up an Eisteddfod at Oban, with a Campbell in the fore-front, shewing that they had not forgotten the old Celtic Institution'.

Mr Mansel Lewis of Stradey Castle stated that the Llanelli Eisteddfod Arts Committee had endeavoured to make the Arts Exhibition 'something far in advance of all previous shows,' but the result was disappointing, and Professor (later Sir) Hubert Herkomer, R.A., the adjudicator, called on the Eisteddfod authorities to 'make the art section as important as they had made music.' Herkomer was the son of a Bavarian wood-carver, who had been educated in England and had settled in London in 1870. In 1889, he was appointed Slade professor at Oxford, and he later set up his own school of art in Bushey, where he established himself as a portrait painter and engraver. He was elected a Royal Academician in 1890 and he received a knighthood in 1907. His wife was Welsh and he was a close friend of the Mansel Lewis family.

The Crown was awarded to Llew Llwyfo for his poem *Ioan y Disgybl Annwyl* (John the dear disciple). He was escorted to the platform by bardic officials in their Gorsedd robes, and the crown was placed on his head by Mrs Trubshaw of Llanelli. The Chair, awarded for an *awdl* on *Dedwyddwch* (Happiness), was won by Pedrog (John Owen Williams : 1853-1932) out of twenty-six entries, the largest number hitherto received. Pedrog, who was a Congregational minister in Liverpool, was unable to be present to receive his award and he was represented by his son.

A contemporary report stated that the 'picturesque appearance of the platform' during the chairing ceremony had been 'considerably heightened since the introduction of Gorseddic robes', which had been designed by Professor Herkomer, in accordance with Iolo Morganwg's injunction that they should be of a uniform and symbolic colour. The robe of the Order of Ovates is green 'to signify the novitiate's growth and increase in learning and science'. The Order of Bards, Musicians and Literati wear a blue robe to signify the sky-blue colour perceptible in serene summer weather, 'as an indication of peace and tranquillity and that all visible things are seen best in that heavenly light'. The Druidic Order's robe is white 'in token of that uncompromising and unsullied Truth which should claim their full allegiance in all their work whether in Art or in Science', in accordance with the motto of that Order, *Y Gwir yn erbyn y Byd* (The Truth against the World).

The Grand Sword was also designed by Herkomer, who explained the symbolism of its parts in a letter to Morien (Owen Morgan : 1836-1921) : 'The natural crystal in the hilt stands for mystery. Within it are drilled the three sacred lines supposed to be the first attempt to write Jehovah, the dragon guarding both. The hand-guard is of wrought steel, the dragon and handle of copper gilt. The scabbard being of wood, symbolises peace. On the five bands that encircle the scabbard will be found embossed the words 'Y Gwir yn erbyn y byd, Duw a phob daioni, Calon wrth galon, A laddo a leddir, Iesu na ad gamwaith' (The truth against the world; God and all goodness; Heart to heart; He who kills shall be killed; Jesus let no oppression persist: the mottoes of the five provinces of Wales: Morgannwg and Gwent, Gwynedd, Powys, and Dyfed)'. This letter is quoted by Maxwell Fraser, wife of the Archdruid Trefin (1960-62), in her all-embracing, two-volume work, *Wales*, where she also quotes how Morton Nance, the Grand Bard of Cornwall, 'recalled that he saw the (Archdruid's) crown of oak-leaves and acorns being made when he was a student at Bushey under Sir Hubert, with a spray of oak beside it, from which it was copied in metal, and a copy of an ancient British breastplate and a crystal-headed sceptre to go with it.'

At the Gorsedd ceremony held in Happy Valley to open the 1896 Eisteddfod at Llandudno, Sir Arthur Stepney ascended the Logan Stone, dressed in the green robe of an Ovate, and presented the Archdruid Hwfa Môn with an embroidered Banner for the Gorsedd of Bards. The Banner had been designed by the Herald Bard, Arlunydd Pen-y-garn and comprised a sky-blue background embroidered in gold with oak leaves, leeks and mistletoe. On its upper part is a rampant dragon in the centre of a radiant sun, three rays of which form the mystic sign, and between the rays are woven the Gorsedd mottoes: *Yng ngwyneb haul llygad goleuni* (In the face of the sun, the eye of light) and *Y Gwir yn erbyn y Byd*. In the lower half is a circle of crystals, representing the Gorsedd Circle, in which is inscribed the word *Heddwch*. The Banner was made by Lena Evans (Brodes Dâr).

Arlunydd Pen-y-garn had also made the original suggestion for the design of the Hirlas Horn which was executed by Sir William Goscombe John, R.A., from the horn of a Cape Buffalo. The Horn has a silver cover surmounted by a druid carrying a harp and surrounded by five dragons curled round semi-precious stones, and on its side is a silver shield bearing the arms of its donor, Lord Tredegar. The Horn rests on a stand consisting of a massive silver dragon holding in its claws a large crystal.

The silver crown offered at the Blaenau Ffestiniog Eisteddfod of 1898 for a *pryddest* on *Thomas Charles o'r Bala* was awarded, in his absence, to Gwylfa Roberts. Elfyn (R. O. Hughes : 1858-1919) won the chair for his *awdl* on *Awen* (Muse) and was chaired at a ceremony attended by the Duke of Cambridge, the Prince of Saxe-Weimar, Lord Carrington, Lord Colville and others.

The unexpectedly fine weather and sunshine at the notoriously rainy Blaenau Ffestiniog, caused Dyfed to proclaim his astonishment in *cynghanedd:* 'Bu'r Wyl heb ambarelo' (There was not an umbrella at the festival).

The Cardiff Eisteddfod of 1899 may best be remembered for the presence of representatives from other Celtic countries. A large delegation from Brittany, headed by Taldir Jaffrennou, the Breton poet, and Anatole le Braz, the author of *Land of the Pardons*, discussed the idea of establishing a Breton branch of the Gorsedd of Bards of the Isle of Britain and, as a result, *Gorsedd Llydaw*, the Gorsedd of the Bards of Brittany, was founded in the following year. From the beginning of the nineteenth century there had been a desire to establish close links between Brittany and Wales, largely through the efforts of Ar Gonidec, who had sought refuge in this country when his Breton nationality was threatened after the French Revolution, and who had come under the influence of the cultural awakening in Wales. He returned to Brittany and succeeded in creating a Breton literary language, despite all efforts to suppress it by the French. The inspiration for a Breton Gorsedd grew out of this revival, and from the efforts of Carnhuanawc (Thomas Price : 1787-1848), who had promoted the translation of the scriptures into Breton and suggested the formation of a Cambro-Breton literary society and the holding of a Breton eisteddfod as early as 1829, and also from the enthusiasm of the Vicomte de la Villemarqué (1815-95), the 'inventor' of Breton folksongs, who was the first Breton to attend an Eisteddfod, at Abergavenny in 1838.

The Breton deputation appeared under a banner bearing the ducal ermine of Brittany and its leader presented to the Archdruid the Welsh half of the split sword which is conjoined with the Breton half at joint Gorsedd ceremonies as 'a symbol of the spiritual unity of King Arthur's sword between the Welsh and Breton nations'.

Cornwall was also represented at Cardiff, and the Cornish historian, J. Hobson Matthews, was installed as a member of the Gorsedd under the name Mab Cernyw (the son of Cornwall). The close contact with Cornish men of letters remained, with Henry Jenner (Gwaz Mikael) admitted to the Gorsedd in 1904, along with the founder of the Celtic-Cornish Society, Duncombe Jewell (Bardd Glas), and although the possibility of instituting a Cornish Gorsedd was considered on more than one occasion, *Gorseth Kernow* was not established until 1928, with Jenner as Grand Bard. Like the Breton Gorsedd, it had complete autonomy in its own affairs, but each recognised the Archdruid and the Welsh Gorsedd as the supreme authority, and their ritual and costumes were modelled on those of Gorsedd y Beirdd with minor adaptations.

Ireland was represented at the Cardiff Eisteddfod by the twenty-year old Irish patriot Padraig Pearse, who was invited to speak from the Maen Llog and initiated a member of the Gorsedd of Bards.

No Gorsedd has been established in Ireland or in Scotland or the Isle of Man, but delegates from these countries regularly visit the Eisteddfod and thus maintain contact between the Celtic countries of Goidelic origin and those of Brythonic stock.

Eisteddfod Cadair Ddu Birkenhead at which the Chair was draped in black when it was learnt that the winning bard, Hedd Wyn, was killed in action in France in 1917.

HRH The Prince of Wales (later King Edward VIII) with Sir Vincent Evans, the Secretary of the Eisteddfod, and the Archdruid Elfed at the Swansea Eisteddfod of 1926.

John Masefield with the Archdruid Gwili and the Crowned Bard Simon B. Jones at the Wrexham Eisteddfod of 1933.

The Archdruid J.J. and the Herald Bard (Captain Geoffrey Crawshay) at the Fishguard Eisteddfod of 1936.

HRH Prince Charles, the Prince of Wales, greeted by the author at the Flint Eisteddfod of 1969.

The Crowning Ceremony at the Haverfordwest Eisteddfod of 1972.

The opening of a Gorsedd Ceremony, with the unsheathing of the Grand Sword.

The bearer of the Hirlas horn and the blodeuged.

THE TWENTIETH CENTURY

Brilliant sunshine shone on the Gorsedd ceremony held in the Whitley Gardens to open the Liverpool Eisteddfod in 1900. The procession leading to it was headed by the band of H.M.S. *Indefatigable,* followed by the Gorsedd Banner and the Hirlas Horn. M. Radiquet, representing Brittany, carried the Breton half-sword. The Lord Mayor of Liverpool, (the Right Hon. Louis S. Cohen), was received by the Archdruid, Hwfa Môn, on the Logan Stone and admitted to the bardic circle under the name *Cohenydd*!

The Eisteddfod was held at the North Haymarket in a pavilion decorated with flags and banners; the walls hung with portraits of bardic celebrities. The Lord Mayor presided over the opening ceremony, supported on the platform by the Bards in their robes. The Hirlas Horn and the Grand Sword were placed before him and the Gorsedd Banner behind his chair.

The Eisteddfod returned to Merthyr Tydfil in 1901, and it was opened at a Gorsedd Ceremony held at Cwm-pen-coedcae on the morning of Tuesday, 6 August.

The variety of interests provided for Eisteddfod-goers is revealed in the programme which announced competitions in Chemistry, Entomology, Weaving, Knitting, Crocheting, Embroidery, Needlework, Photography, Modelling, Sculpture, Oil Painting, Water Colours, First-Aid, Geology, Wood Carving, Agriculture, Mining, Architecture, Pottery, Basketry, Bookbinding and Botany — (a 'collection of Poisonous Plants found in Wales'.) These, of course, were included in addition to choral contests and solo competitions — pianoforte, penillion, harp, flute, violin, vocal; and competitions in literature and poetry.

The Honourable Society of Cymmrodorion Section held meetings at the Merthyr Town Hall at which papers were read on subjects such as 'National Health', 'Sanitation in Wales', and 'The Welsh Language and how to preserve it out of Wales': the latter being promoted jointly by the Cymmrodorion and the newly-formed Welsh Language Society.

The Annual Joint Meeting of the Gorsedd and the Eisteddfod Association expressed its grief at the death of the president, the third Marquess of Bute, and appointed the fourth Marquess as his successor. The Hon. Mrs Bulkeley Owen (Gwenrhian Gwynedd) moved a resolution 'calling attention to the deplorable state of art competitions at the Eisteddfod' and suggested that 'means should be devised to raise the tone of the exhibitions, by appointing a committee, withholding the prizes, or by some other means'. She strongly objected to giving prizes for imitation art. 'Why paint their native slate to imitate marble? And why grain wood to imitate oak while they had the noble tree available? (Cheers).' The Herald Bard, Arlunydd Pen-y-garn, seconded the resolution and reminded the meeting of the appeal made by Professor Hubert Herkomer, at the Llanelli Eisteddfod of 1895, for an improvement in the standard of the art exhibitions. The Eisteddfod Association offered a gold medal designed by Sir William Goscombe John to encourage competition in the arts.

The Bangor Eisteddfod of 1902 was opened with a Gorsedd ceremony held on Maesylleiniau (now the Bangor City Football Ground) at 9 o'clock on the morning of Tuesday, 9 September, and there were similar ceremonies held on the Thursday and Friday mornings, 'within a circle of unhewn stones . . . guarded by twelve Bards placed one by each stone and two Keepers of the Gate stationed at the entrance'.

In *The Transactions of the Bangor Eisteddfod* it states that 'the Archdruid presides over the ceremonies and occupies the centre of the Logan Stone. All Wales is divided into five 'Chairs', or Provinces and each 'Chair' has its own proper motto. The motto of the Gorsedd of All Britain is 'Truth against the world'. That of *Gwynedd* (North Wales) is 'O Jesus, permit no wrong'. The motto of *Powys* is 'The slayer shall be slain'; of *Dyfed* (Pembroke), 'Heart to heart'; of Glamorgan, 'God and all goodness'; and of *Caerleon,* 'Under the protection of God and his Peace'. All laws for the regulation of Bardism, before they come into force, must be recited publicly in the Gorsedd on three separate occasions, with an interval of one year between the several recitals, and if approved become valid, and cannot be changed or altered without going through the same process. The Gorsedd holds annual examinations in Poetry and Music, and the successful candidates are admitted to its Degrees, and invested in the open Gorsedd.'

Some three thousand onlookers had gathered at Maesylleiniau, to witness the Menai Bridge band lead in the procession of Bards, who had donned their robes of white, blue and green in the

Magistrates Court-room. The Archdruid, Hwfa Môn, was supported on the arms of Ap Caledfryn (William Williams : 1837-1915), and Cochfarf (Edward Thomas : 1853-1912), the Grand Sword Bearer. The Gorsedd prayer was offered by Professor Witton Davies and a fanfare was sounded on the *Corn Gwlad,* the official Gorsedd trumpet. The *Aberthged* (a sheaf of wild flowers and fruits of the earth) was presented to the Archdruid by Cerddores Menai (Mrs Hunter of Plas Coch) and the Hirlas Horn by Mrs Yale on behalf of the Mayoress of Bangor (Mrs Henry Lewis). A deputation from Ireland, including A. P. Graves, the author of 'Father O'Flynn', was introduced to the Archdruid, along with a representative of the Cornish Bardic Society. The Marquess of Anglesey was admitted to the Gorsedd, and Lord Mostyn announced that he had received a telegram from Queen Marie of Rumania which read: 'My congratulations and best wishes for the success of my dear Eisteddfod. Carmen Sylva.'

The Cymmrodorion Section met to continue the discussions which had begun at the Merthyr Eisteddfod the previous year on 'National Health' and 'Sanitation in Wales'.

There was seating for ten thousand people in the pavilion erected in Ffordd y Garth, and every seat was taken in time to hear the Chief Choral competition. Of the nine choirs competing, six were from England — Shrewsbury, The Potteries, Huddersfield, North Staffordshire, Blackpool, and the Isle of Man. The competition lasted four and a half hours and North Staffordshire won the prize. The audience demanded that the adjudication be given in Welsh and several times during the Eisteddfod revealed their concern at the extent to which the Eisteddfod had been anglicized. There was not a single item in Welsh listed in the programme of the evening concert and when Miss Clara Williams sang *Y Deryn Pur* as an encore, she received a deafening ovation from the audience of seven thousand people.

Lord Castletown, in presiding over Wednesday's proceedings, stated that the Irish people regarded it a great honour that he should have been invited to preside. He thanked the Archdruid and the members of the Gorsedd who had crossed to Ireland to attend a meeting of the Pan-Celtic League, and he was pleased to observe that the banners of the Celtic nations had been displayed in the pavilion.

At the annual general meeting of the Gorsedd, Mr Beriah Gwynfe Evans reminded his audience that no Eisteddfod could be held without the consent of the Gorsedd, and that the Gorsedd had jurisdiction over the local committees, especially insofar as the choice of subjects for competitions was concerned. The Rev. Peris Williams conveyed greetings from the Druids of Germany who asked if they could become affiliated to *Gorsedd y Beirdd*. It was decided that the German Gorsedd be invited to send representatives to discuss the matter.

Professor Hugh Johnson, a linguist from Egypt, was received into the Order of Bards under the bardic name 'Moses'. The Archdruid stated that as Professor Johnson was a lawyer by profession, he had chosen for his bardic title the name of the archlawyer who had received the tablets of the law on Mount Sinai!

The President for the Thursday afternoon session was Mr David Lloyd George, M.P., who expressed his pleasure in finding that a choir from America would be competing that day. There was an old saying 'Môr o gân yw Cymru i gyd' (All Wales is a sea of song), but the waves of that sea had driven over Offa's Dyke, and the prizes had gone to Blackpool and the Black Country. He criticized the Welsh people for allowing this to happen and accused them of having set aside their heritage.

The Chair was offered for an *awdl* on *Ymadawiad Arthur* (The Death of Arthur), which was a departure from the biblical and abstract subjects previously favoured. Professor John Morris-Jones and Elfed had adjudicated the ten entrants and Professor Morris-Jones announced that the winner was *Tir na'n Og*. It was revealed that this was the nom-de-plume of T. Gwynn Jones of the *Caernarvon Herald*, but he was unable to be present and Beriah Gwynfe Evans acted as his proxy. This was the first of the great Eisteddfodic *awdlau* of this century, but the traditionalists were quick to condemn it as too academic.

At the joint annual meeting of the Gorsedd and the National Eisteddfod Association, Mr Robert Bryan, inviting the 1904 Eisteddfod to Wrexham, stated that lovers of the Eisteddfod had been revolted by the anglicized attitude of the people of Bangor and promised that if the Eisteddfod came to Wrexham, this matter would be remedied. The Wrexham deputation, however, was not prepared to share any profits with the Eisteddfod Association and The Gorsedd, and wanted them to be devoted to local charities. They were informed that this condition was not acceptable and it was decided that the 1904 Eisteddfod should be held at Rhyl.

Hwfa Môn died at Rhyl in November 1905, having held the office of Archdruid for a period of ten years. He did much to uphold the traditions of Gorsedd y Beirdd, believing firmly in its antiquity. He was a fluent preacher and speaker, but had a tendency for prolixity.

He was succeeded by Dyfed (Evan Rees : 1850-1923) a native of Puncheston in Pembrokeshire. His parents moved to Aberdare when he was a child and he was employed at Blaen-gwawr colliery by the time he was eight years of age. He became a Calvinistic Methodist minister and travelled over the five continents as a lecturer. He was a successful competitor at eisteddfodau having won the Chair at Merthyr Tydfil (1881), Liverpool (1884), Brecon (1889), and again at Merthyr in 1901. In 1893 he won the prize, — the most valuable ever offered to a Welsh poet, — at the International Eisteddfod held at the World Fair in Chicago. He was installed Archdruid at the Caernarfon Eisteddfod in 1906 and was the last to retain the office for life.

The Chair at the Caernarfon Eisteddfod was awarded to J. J. Williams for his memorable *awdl 'Y Lloer'* (The Moon).

At the Llangollen Eisteddfod of 1908, Gorsedd ceremonies were held on the mornings of Tuesday, Thursday and Friday, 1, 3 and 4 September, at Plas Newydd; and in addition to the Annual General Meeting, members were summoned to a special meeting at Capel Seion vestry to consider the third reading of the new rules put forward by the Gorsedd Committee. Membership of the Gorsedd was to be confined to those who had passed the examinations appropriate to the Order of Ovate, Bard or Musician, except for those Ovates and Druids awarded degrees by the Gorsedd Committee. Examination centres were to be established throughout Wales and in some English towns, at which examinations would be held three months prior to the Eisteddfod. It was agreed that the Chair should continue to be offered as the prize for an *awdl;* and the Crown for an *arwrgerdd* (heroic poem) the one to be regarded equal to the other, as recommended by the Gorsedd at the Carmarthen Eisteddfod in 1867. It was emphasized that no language save Welsh would be spoken or used in Gorsedd meetings or ceremonies.

The last decision was taken seriously by the promoters of the 1909 Eisteddfod at London. The programme for the proclamation ceremony was wholly in Welsh, including literal translations of place names; for example, the robing room for the Gorsedd members was 'yn neuadd y Deml Fewnol allan o Heol y Chwern-nant yn Ninas Caerludd' (in the Inner Temple hall off Fleet Street in the City of London). The ceremony was held in the gardens of the Inner Temple on *Alban Hefin* (10 June), and Lord Aberdare presided over a Proclamation Banquet in the evening at which the Archdruid and the Gorsedd members were present.

The Albert Hall was the venue of the London Eisteddfod,

following a Gorsedd ceremony held in Kensington Gardens. The Annual Joint Meeting of the Gorsedd and the Eisteddfod Association, also held at the Albert Hall, had an unprecedented attendance consisting mainly of supporters from each of the towns applying for the 1911 Eisteddfod. These were Abergavenny and Carmarthen, between which there had been a lively rivalry for the honour, and the membership of the Association had benefitted as a result. Carmarthen stressed 'its Eisteddfodic associations from 1461 *(sic)* onward' and Abergavenny appealed for the Eisteddfod to 'ratify the conquest of Monmouthshire by Wales'. The Rt. Hon. Reginald McKenna, M.P., First Lord of the Admiralty, supporting Lord Tredegar and Lord Aberdare, said that there were 'still unlettered persons in the House of Commons who were wont to speak of Wales and Monmouthshire as if they were separate entities (laughter). Let them take the National Eisteddfod to Abergavenny and thus prove that Gwent is Wales (applause).' Despite the plea, Abergavenny received the support of only 91 members, while 142 voted in favour of Carmarthen.

The Honorary Secretary, E. Vincent Evans, had to report that the anticipated profit of £600 from the Swansea Eisteddfod of 1907 turned out to be a loss of £60; but the Llangollen Eisteddfod, despite the inclement weather, had shown a profit of £140, half of which had been remitted to the Association in accordance with the agreed policy.

The presidents of the day at the London Eisteddfod included A. J. Balfour, David Lloyd George, (then Chancellor of the Exchequer), and H. H. Asquith, the Prime Minister.

The Chair for the best *awdl* to *Gwlad y Bryniau* (The Land of the Hills) which attracted twenty-one entries, (one of which was in English), was awarded to T. Gwynn Jones who, as in 1902, had written an outstanding ode. There were only six aspirants for the Crown offered for a *pryddest* on *Yr Arglwydd Rhys* and 'Mr W. J. Gruffydd, M.A., Bethel, (later Professor W. J. Gruffydd), was crowned in accordance with the ceremonies of the Bards by the Archdruid and the Officers of the Gorseddic Circle'. The prize of £5 for 'a Soprano Song to the words *Ynys y Plant,* by Elfed,' drew nineteen entries and was won by E. T. Davies of Dowlais.

The Colwyn Bay Eisteddfod of 1910 produced an *awdl* which was among the finest ever written — *Yr Haf* (The Summer) by R. Williams Parry. At Wrexham in 1912, his cousin, T. H. Parry Williams, became the first poet to win both the chair and the crown at the same Eisteddfod — with his *awdl* to *Y Mynydd* (The Mountain) and his *pryddest* to *Gerallt Gymro.*

In *Y Beirniad* published in 1911 Sir John Morris-Jones, an ardent commentator on the organisation of the Eisteddfod from 1896 onwards, launched an attack on the Gorsedd, charging it with being 'a recent device founded on fiction and deceit' and accusing its leaders of polluting the sources of history and of misleading 'the poor Bretons who have been so naïve as to imitate them'.

The Annual Meeting held during the Carmarthen Eisteddfod of 1911 was thronged with supporters from the towns of Aberdare, Abergavenny, Aberystwyth and Barry, all of which sought the honour of inviting the 1913 event. The High Constable of Aberdare, Mr Frank Hodges, led his town's deputation in the absence of Lord Merthyr. The Mayor of Aberystwyth, Capt. Fossett Roberts, reminded members that the Eisteddfod had not been held in mid-Wales since 1865 and that Aberystwyth was making its third application. Barry and Aberdare withdrew their applications after the first vote had been taken, and Abergavenny was eventually selected.

The local nobility featured largely among the presidents of the day at Carmarthen and included Sir Courtenay Mansel, Sir Marteine Lloyd, Sir James Drummond, Lady St David's and Sir Owen Philipps (later Lord Kylsant).

The Cymmrodorion Section devoted its sessions, at the Carmarthen Town Hall, to discussions on 'The Organization of Welsh Historical and Archaeological Research' and 'Housing Conditions in Wales'. In his paper on the latter, Dr D. L. Thomas, the Medical Officer of Health for Stepney, advocated the establishment of garden cities throughout the principality.

With the outbreak of war in 1914, it was felt necessary to postpone the Eisteddfod which had been proclaimed and arranged to take place at Bangor.

Bangor received the event, however, in 1915, but with a modified programme, and the local organizing committee was greatly praised for its endeavours. Elfed, in moving a resolution to express the Association's debt of gratitude to the Bangor Committee, thought that the railways could have given more assistance by running excursions. Mr David Lloyd George, recently appointed Minister of Munitions, was quick to point out that the railways had been taken over by the Government. If excursions had been run to Bangor people would have said 'Lloyd George did it.' He averred that 'there was no need to abandon the Eisteddfod because of the war. Welshmen wished to hear the music of the harp above the din of battle. "Business as usual" for the Welsh muse!' He suggested that the festival should be simplified and curtailed, and appealed to Aberystwyth to provide it with a home the following year.

The Eisteddfod Association mourned the loss of Sir Marchant Williams who had died in October. Born the son of a coal miner at Aberdare, he had been one of the first students of the new University College of Wales at Aberystwyth and had worked as a school teacher and inspector of schools before taking up law and being called to the bar at the age of 40. When the National Eisteddfod Society was established in 1880, Marchant Williams was invited to become its honorary secretary. He later became its chairman and remained in that office until his death, when W. Llewelyn Williams, K.C., the Member of Parliament for the Carmarthen boroughs, was elected chairman in his place.

The Crown and the Chair had been won by the same poet for the first time at the Wrexham Eisteddfod in 1912. The poet, T. H. Parry-Williams, had submitted the poems from Freiberg University, where he was a student and, on the morning of the crowning ceremony, which was Wednesday at that time, he had cycled to the Eisteddfod from the Vale of Clwyd where he was spending his holiday on his uncle's farm. His pseudonym had been called from the Eisteddfod platform for the second time before he heard it, and he had to be lifted over a barrier by his bardic escort before he could be conducted to the stage. He was chaired the next day.

T. H. Parry-Williams repeated his outstanding performance in 1915, at the Bangor Eisteddfod. He was not present at the crowning ceremony: he was haymaking at his uncle's farm in the Vale of Clwyd and the Crown was received by his father on his behalf, but he presented himself at Bangor the next day for the chairing ceremony. He had written his *awdl* to *Eryri* (Snowdonia) while he was a student at the Sorbonne during the winter of 1913 for submission at the Eisteddfod planned for 1914, but his *pryddest* to *Y Ddinas* (The City) was not written until he returned to Aberystwyth, and in it he described the more salacious side of Parisian life.

For the first time a prize was offered for the performance of a play. Play-acting had been regarded as sinful in Nonconformist Wales and otherwise upright people had been excommunicated for having taken part in plays. The Llanberis Eisteddfod had offered a prize in 1879 for 'a Welsh drama after the style of Shakespeare' at the request of a group of local quarrymen who discussed Shakespearian plays at work and, on winter evenings, at the home of the local shopkeeper, and performed excerpts in summer on the banks of Llyn Padarn.

The winning play, *Owain Glyndŵr* by Beriah Gwynfe Evans, had been performed at Llanberis in 1880 and was the first full-length play to be written in Welsh.

'Cadair Ddu Birkenhead' is synonymous with tragedy in the minds of all Welshmen. The subject for the Chair at the Eisteddfod held in that town in 1917 was *Yr Arwr* (The Hero). When the pseudonym of the winner, 'Fleur-de-lis', was called by the Archdruid, it was disclosed that the poet had been killed in France.

The poet was Hedd Wyn (Ellis Humphrey Evans) born at Yr Ysgwrn, Trawsfynydd, on 13 January 1887. After a spasmodic elementary education, he worked for a while in South Wales but was not happy there and remained at home as a shepherd until he enlisted in the 15th Bn. the Royal Welch Fusiliers early in 1917. He had won prizes at eisteddfodau from an early age and, at the Aberystwyth Eisteddfod of 1916 his *awdl, Ystrad Fflur* (Strata Florida) was placed second to that of J. Ellis Williams.

The hero of his *awdl* at Birkenhead was Prometheus. He had written part of the poem before joining the Army, had completed it in camp at Litherland, and posted it from France where he was killed in action at the battle of Pilkem Ridge on 31 July 1917. When no one responded to the Archdruid's call, the Chair of Birkenhead was draped in black, and has since been known as 'Cadair Ddu Birkenhead'.

The former Archdruid William Morris, a boyhood friend of Hedd Wyn, who had taught him some of the rules of prosody and had loaned him books on Prometheus, recalls the mournful scene in Dyfed's words 'Yr wyl yn ei dagrau, a'r bardd yn ei fedd' (The festival in its tears, and the poet in his grave). Hedd Wyn's name became a household word, and the tragedy of his death has been immortalised in a chain of poignant and beautiful *englynion* by R. Williams Parry.

At the Eisteddfod held at Neath in 1918, Henry Jenner, the Cornish scholar who had been received into the Gorsedd at Rhyl in 1904, discussed with Beili Glas (D. Rhys Phillips) the idea of forming a Cornish Gorsedd of Bards on the lines of the Breton Gorsedd, to which he had been admitted in 1903 under the name 'Gwaz Mikael'.

The chair was won at Neath by J. T. Job, who had previously won it at Newport, Mon., in 1897 for his *Brawdgarwch* (Brotherly Love), and at Llanelli in 1903 for *Y Celt* (The Celt). The subject at Neath was *Eu Nêr a Folant* (Their God they worship), a line from an early poem, the initials of which the poet took to name his son, Enaf.

Hitherto, the Eisteddfod had been held at random dates, usually between June and September, with a growing tendency towards the early part of the latter month. In 1918 the Eisteddfod Association decided to adopt the first week in August as a permanent date for the festival.

The Caernarfon Eisteddfod of 1921 made a great contribution to Welsh literature by producing two outstanding poems; Meuryn's *awdl, Min y Môr* (The Edge of the Sea), and a *pryddest* by Cynan to *Mab y Bwthyn* (The Cotter's Son), which gave a candid statement of his experiences as a soldier in France during the war.

Cynan won the Crown again in 1923, at Mold, for *Yr Ynys Unig* (The Lonely Isle) and, in the following year at Pontypool, he received the Chair for his poem *I'r Duw Nid Adwaenir* (To the Unknown God) which broke with tradition for it was written in mesur y tri thrawiad' (the measure of the three beats) which was not among the twenty-four measures of Dafydd ab Edmwnd permitted to be used in the composition of an *awdl*. The Crown was awarded at Pontypool to Prosser Rhys for his *Atgof* (Memory), an uninhibited poem dealing with the problems of a sensuous young man. This caused a considerable raising of eyebrows and the inevitable protests in the press.

Since the beginning of the century *Gorsedd y Beirdd* had been the target of much criticism by some prominent Welshmen, led by Sir John Morris-Jones, Professor of Welsh at the University College of North Wales, Bangor. These attacks were renewed in 1922 by Griffith John Williams who alleged that 'such was the pomposity and arrogance of the Gorsedd that it regarded itself as the literary court of justice in Wales.' He was unable to commend it as a pageant even, but he could see a future for it as a kind of academy which could produce a school of critics in Wales.

Professor Henry Lewis entered the arena in 1926 when he accused the Gorsedd of general incompetence and interference with the local committee's selection of subjects and adjudicators, but he acknowledged that there were efforts being made towards its reform. His attack drew a reply from Cynan who discarded the theories relating to the antiquity of the Gorsedd and its druidic connection, and emphasized the contribution it was making, and could make, to the Eisteddfod.

At the same time Professor W. J. Gruffydd began his 'Editorial Notes' in *Y Llenor* with the disarming statement: 'It would be futile for us to assume that everyone in Wales is perfectly satisfied with the old institution or with that which it produces, although that has improved immensely during this century, but for better or for worse, the Eisteddfod has by now become a part of the national life, and it is our duty to make it as worthy of that life as we can.'

Gruffydd, who was described by Sir Idris Bell as 'something of an *enfant terrible* in Welsh letters, continually in hot water with those whose idea of patriotism is to turn a blind eye to national shortcomings,' was impatient with the amateurism of the organization of the Eisteddfod and persistently attacked the local organising committees for their inexpertise. He appealed to the Gorsedd to bring together, at the Liverpool Eisteddfod in 1929, the leaders of the Welsh nation who were outside its ranks in order to make a concerted effort to establish an efficient governing body for the Eisteddfod before the local committees would complete its demise as a cultural institution. The meeting was duly arranged but Gruffydd himself was unable to be present and nothing was achieved except that some of the promising young poets who had hitherto been disinclined to become members of the Gorsedd, although entitled to be admitted as winners of the Chair or the Crown, now came forward to be initiated.

Gruffydd renewed his appeal for action following the Llanelli Eisteddfod of 1930, maintaining that the local organizing committee was unaware 'that any progress had taken place in Welsh literature since about 1885.' He now asked Sir Vincent Evans to call a joint meeting of the Gorsedd and of the Eisteddfod Council in an effort to bring about some improvement. But those who held power in both of these bodies were conservative in their ideas, and there was little hope of reform while they remained in harness.

The Eisteddfod visited Anglesey in 1927, being held at Holyhead. No one was deemed worthy of the Chair for an ode to *Y Derwydd* (The Druid) but the Crown was awarded to Caradog Prichard, who relates how he arrived at Holyhead, his first Eisteddfod, having been given a hint and nothing more, that his *pryddest* to *Y Briodas* (The Wedding) had been successful. On the Monday evening he was sitting in the lounge of the Railway Hotel 'gazing in awe at some of the giants around me — giants like Gwallter Dyfi, the Grand Sword-bearer, and Sieffre o Gyfarthfa who rides a horse at the head of the Gorsedd procession, and many another national figure. I was listening amazed at the gaiety and laughter and the noisy carousal around me, when suddenly a voice from behind me whispered in my ear: "Wylwch, y ffyliaid, chwerthwch ..." (Weep, you fools, laugh).' This was a line from the poem he had submitted for the Crown, and the whisper came from R. Williams Parry who was one of the adjudicators. Caradog knew immediately that the Crown was his.

The Chair which could find no worthy poet became the Judge's chair in the Beaumaris Assize Court.

Caradog Prichard won the Crown for the second year running at the Treorci Eisteddfod in 1928 for a *pryddest* to *Penyd* (Penance). For the second year in succession also, the Chair was withheld as the adjudicators considered no one worthy of the prize for an *awdl* to *Y Sant* (The Saint), but few people agreed with Sir John Morris-Jones's savage indictment that Gwenallt, in his entry, was 'wallowing in lust'.

At a meeting of the Federation of Old Cornwall Societies in 1927, Henry Jenner brought forward the idea of establishing a Cornish Gorsedd, on the pattern of the Breton one. The idea was approved by the Federation and a petition was sent to the Archdruid Pedrog and *Gorsedd y Beirdd*. The proposal was warmly received and, as a first step, a nucleus of eight Cornishmen was initiated at the Treorci Eisteddfod in 1928. In September of that year, the Archdruid, accompanied by Gorsedd leaders including Elfed, Beili Glas and Meurig Prysor (Canon Maurice Jones, Principal of Lampeter College) travelled to Boscawen-Un to establish *Gorseth Kernow* and to install Henry Jenner as the first Grand Bard of Cornwall.

The Cornish ceremony is an adaptation of that of *Gorsedd y Beirdd* and is held in a different place each year, often within a pre-historic stone circle. The Cornish bards all wear blue robes with a head-band of black and gold, and the Grand Bard is adorned with a laurel wreath and a breastplate, both of beaten copper. The Cornish banner bears the symbol of the three shafts of light within a border of Cornish besants.

The 1929 Eisteddfod held at Liverpool was the last to be staged outside Wales. The fact that it was a financial loss did not encourage the Eisteddfod authorities to cross the border again.

The Chair was won at Liverpool by Dewi Emrys (David Emrys James : 1881-1952), 'the vagabond poet, who wandered from place to place ... emerging only on those occasions of important Eisteddfodau', and who had won the Crown at the Swansea Eisteddfod of 1926 for a collection of poems, *Rhigymau'r Ffordd Fawr* (Rhymes of the Open Road), and had immediately pledged it with a Swansea pawnbroker. The subject for the Chair was *Dafydd ap Gwilym,* and Dewi's poem received high praise from the adjudicators, one of whom went so far as to suggest that the 'empty

90

Chairs' of previous eisteddfodau should be awarded to the poet as well. Dewi, however, wrote to Trefin (Edgar Phillips: 1889-1962), whose poem had been rated third in the competition by the adjudicators, to say that he considered Trefin's to be the best and that his own was nothing more than a piecing together of two of his earlier poems 'but the fools (the adjudicators) could not see that.' Wil Ifan, one of the adjudicators of the *pryddest* on *Y Gân ni Chanwyd* (The Song that was not Sung), wanted to award the Crown to Dewi Emrys also, but his co-judges voted in favour of the poem submitted by Caradog Prichard, who thus won the Crown for the third year in succession.

Dewi Emrys won the Chair again, the following year at Llanelli for an *awdl* on *Y Galilead* (The Galilean). When the Archdruid, Pedrog, called on the successful poet to stand, there was no response. It had been whispered that Dewi was the winner, but he had appeared on the Eisteddfod platform with all the other bards at the commencement of the chairing ceremony. Just before the pseudonym of the winner was announced, however, he had left the platform unobserved and had joined the multitude on the field, whence he was eventually retrieved and brought unwillingly into the pavilion and onto the stage. He later admitted that he had acted thus in protest against not being officially informed of his success, and he was only persuaded to conform when he was told that Mr Lloyd George would be upset if the ceremony would be marred by his reluctance to be chaired. Dewi was undoubtedly also registering his protest against 'the establishment', which found it difficult to accept on equal terms a person who, though gifted, had chosen to lead a vagrant life and who was frequently on the fringe of breaking the law, and ever in conflict with it.

In 1931, Gwylfa (Gwylfa Roberts) was appointed Recorder of the Gorsedd in succession to Gwilym Rhug. Gwylfa was a native of Penmaenmawr and, after studying at the denominational college at Bangor, he became a Congregational Minister first at Port Dinorwic and then, for thirty-six years, at Tabernacl, Llanelli. He had been awarded the Crown for his ode to *Charles o'r Bala* at the Blaenau Ffestiniog Eisteddfod in 1898, and also at Cardiff in the following year for his *Y Diddanydd Arall* (The Other Comforter).

The Eisteddfod held at Bangor in that year was attended by H. V. Morton, who was touring North Wales gathering material for his book *In Search of Wales* in which he wrote: 'The National Eisteddfod is, I think, one of the most interesting ceremonies I have ever attended. I have seen kings crowned and I have seen them buried. I have seen nations in mourning and in times of popular rejoicing. I have seen crowds as big as this Welsh crowd whipped up into a dervish frenzy about sport; but never have I seen a crowd which represents all the lights and shades of an entire nation gathered together to sing, to play musical instruments and to recite verse.'

He arrived early at the opening ceremony of the Gorsedd, held in a meadow on the slope below the University, in time to see a young man in plus-fours enter the circle of stones bearing a bunch of green leaves with which he proceeded to conceal a microphone placed on the Maen Llog. The Bards filed into the circle and he noted that 'now and again the irreverent wind blows aside the robes to reveal trousers of serge and tweed and pin-stripe ... Father Christmas has the same trouble with his trousers.'

The Eisteddfod was held in 'an enormous wooden pavilion erected on the edge of the Menai Straits,' which Morton entered during a brass band competition. He was 'amused by the elaborate precautions which are taken to ensure that there shall be no favouritism in the judging of brass bands. One of the first require-ments is that the judge shall not be aware of the identity of the band to which he is listening. He is therefore hidden from sight in a green sentry-box. As soon as he is concealed, the bands draw lots for the order of their appearance. A shrill whistle from the hidden judge calls them on the stage one after the other.' The bands were followed by young violinists, then children under eighteen singing *penillion* to the harp. 'The competitions continue all morning. Crowds continually leave and enter the great pavilion. Thousands lie on the grass awaiting their turn to perform.'

On the Tuesday afternoon, Morton himself was sitting on the grass, waiting for the crowning ceremony. He asked a young poet whether the name of the Crowned Bard was really a secret or not. ' "Oh, yes, of course," he replies; then dropping his voice, he says in a mysterious whisper, "I believe it's Cynan. There he is. We'll ask him!" ' But Cynan denied all knowledge.

'The pavilion was packed with people and, in the fulness of time, the Archdruid called on the poet who, according to the adjudicators, had written the best poem on Y Dyrfa (The Crowd) and who bore the nom de plume of "Morgan". At the back of the pavilion a blushing poet rises to his feet. He is a distant indis-tinguishable figure ... The Herald Bard and the Sword Bearer leave the platform and march slowly towards the mysterious "Morgan". They return, one on each side of him, to conduct him to his coronation. No sooner is "Morgan" half down the pavilion that I detect something familiar about him. It *is* Cynan!'

In the evening, Morton attended the Eisteddfod concert and came to the conclusion that 'If you wish to hear singing such as you will hear nowhere else in the world, listen to a mixed choir of Welsh voices. Such singing rouses wonder, admiration and respect. It is no secret that the Welsh have a natural genius for song, but it does seem to me intensely interesting, that this should have been handed down to modern Wales from ancient times. Giraldus Cambrensis, writing in the twelfth century, said of the Welsh: "They do not sing in unison, like the inhabitants of other countries, but in different parts, so that in a company of singers, which one frequently meets with in Wales, as many different parts are heard as there are performers, who at length unite with organic melody in one consonance and soft sweetness of B. Their children from their infancy sing in the same manner!"'

The Chair at the Wrexham Eisteddfod of 1933 was presented by J. R. Jones of Hong Kong, a native of Llanuwchllyn who came each year to attend the National Eisteddfod. It had taken sixteen months for four craftsmen to carve this exquisite piece of Chinese art, depicting scenes and symbols from the ancient fables of China. The Chair was awarded to Trefin who later recorded how he had had difficulty in finding a theme for the set subject, *Harlech*. One evening while the Blackwood Town Military Band was playing in the streets of Blackwood, ('as a tribute to a Welsh poet'), it stopped outside his house and played 'Men of Harlech'. An idea came to him immediately and 'within five minutes I was writing and continued to do so until I nearly collapsed with fatigue.'

From 1880 to 1937 the Eisteddfod was governed on a tri-partite basis: *Cymdeithas yr Eisteddfod* (the Eisteddfod Council), based in London; *Gorsedd Beirdd Ynys Prydain* (no Eisteddfod could be held unless it had been proclaimed at least a year and a day in advance by the Gorsedd); the local organising committee responsible for the local arrangements, and accused by some as being responsible for the lowering standards of the Eisteddfod. Professor Gruffydd claimed that it was 'obvious to every thinking person that the end of the Eisteddfod as a literary institution is at hand unless immediate action is taken to withdraw authority from the local committee.'

The local committee frequently found itself in a situation of divided loyalty, or at least of not knowing which master to serve. In theory, it was responsible to two separate bodies, the Eisteddfod Council and the Gorsedd, between which there was little co-operation or understanding. The Council operated from London, under the dominating leadership of its Secretary, Sir Vincent Evans. Its membership had been reduced to less than thirty, but it had considerable power by virtue of the fact that it held the purse strings. The Gorsedd, with its substantial membership, had made overtures towards reform under the enlightened leadership of its new Archdruid, Gwili, and had expressed its willingness to unite with the Council in order to strengthen the Eisteddfod. The local committees were aware of the weaknesses inherent in this duality, and some of them took advantage of it by introducing local adjudicators of little merit, and by appointing as presidents of the day members of the local squirearchy who were often either unsympathetic or opposed to all things Welsh.

By 1932 it was generally felt that the Eisteddfod was, in the words of Cynan, 'disintegrating through Philistinïsm and parochialism, and that it was high time to make an effort to rebuild it on a strong and proper national basis.' Professor W. J. Gruffydd had returned to the attack. 'The National Eisteddfod is quickly drawing towards its end,' he wrote in *Y Llenor*, 'and the fact that some of us have been prophesying this for some time will not ease the blow when it falls.'

By 1935, the scene was set for change and reform. Cynan had been appointed Recorder of the Gorsedd in succession to Gwylfa, with the express purpose of pursuing the Gorsedd's reforming ideas. It was also necessary to appoint a Secretary to the Eisteddfod Council to succeed Sir Vincent, who had died in the previous year.

Sir Vincent Evans had served as Secretary to the Council, and editor of its publications, since 1881. 'Y Finsent', as he became known, spent his childhood and youth at Trawsfynydd, as a shop assistant and clerk, before going to London in 1872, at the age of twenty, to join the staff of a firm of chartered accountants. He finally became managing director of the Chancery Lane Land and Safe Deposit Company, and took an active part in Welsh cultural life in London. In 1887 he was appointed Secretary of the Honourable Society of Cymmrodorion and later became editor of its *Transactions*. He was appointed president of the Cambrian Archaeological Association and chairman of the Royal Commission on Ancient Monuments. He was knighted in 1909; became High Sheriff of Merioneth in 1919, and was made a Companion of Honour in 1922. For over fifty years, he held a dominant position as Secretary of the Eisteddfod and resisted the attempts that were made from several directions to institute reform.

He was succeeded by D. R. Hughes, a North Walian who had spent years in London and who was eager to make a contribution to Welsh cultural life. The close co-operation between him and

Cynan, and their awareness of the need for reform, ushered a new epoch in the history of the Eisteddfod.

Cynan was a man of tremendous versatility. Hedd Wyn had become the hero-poet of the First War owing to the fact that he had been killed in action before it was proclaimed that he had won the chair at Birkenhead, but he wrote little memorable war poetry; his tenure of the trenches was brief. Cynan, on the other hand, wrote in the mire of Cambrai, in the dugouts of Flanders and the Somme, and the dressing station of 86th Field Ambulance. In Macedonia, 'far too fair for one like me,' he longed for 'the sea-holly and the salty thistle and the strand at Aber-erch', and bid the *nico* (the goldfinch) fly homeward from the banks of the Struma to the garden of Glandŵr, bearing his love, and his *hiraeth* for home, to Megan. He sang in the night in Salonika, and the singing saved him from heartbreak.

He wrote a wealth of high quality poetry on contemporary subjects: his *Mab y Bwthyn* (The Cotter's Son) which won the Crown at Caernarfon in 1921, revealed the soldier's life in France in its reality, the jazz and the tango, the casino and the bistro, the red wine of the Medoc and the blue eyes of Mimi, angel of the *estaminet*. His Crown poem at Bangor in 1931, *Y Dyrfa* (The Crowd), conveyed the excitement of a rugby football match. The *awdl* that won him the Chair at Pontypool in 1924 *I'r Duw Nid Adwaenir* (To the Unknown God), on the other hand, was an example of his ability to write poetry of classic quality.

Cynan was also a supreme actor and producer with a sense of the dramatic that revealed itself in his re-casting of the Gorsedd ceremonies. His voice had a rare power and timbre, and the recordings of it will be preserved for all time. He was an outstanding speaker and raconteur, and no Eisteddfod was complete without a *noson lawen* at which he would perform. He was sensitive, both as a poet and as a person and, despite his many-sided intellectual qualities, he was at all times a man of the people. His conviviality, combined with a tactful but unswerving method of achieving his aims, enabled him to tackle insuperable problems, and succeed.

D. R. Hughes was equally desirous of working for a better understanding between the Eisteddfod Council and the Gorsedd, and of re-establishing the National Eisteddfod as the supreme cultural institution in Wales. He and Cynan brought together the leaders of the two factions at a meeting held at 11, Mecklenburgh Square in London, in 1935, under the impartial chairmanship of David Lloyd George. The meeting adopted a resolution expressing its conviction that there should be one governing body for the National Eisteddfod and urging the appointment of a joint-committee to consider ways and means of achieving this end and to draft a constitution for the new authority, which would merge the Gorsedd and the Eisteddfod Council.

The joint-committee deliberated for a period of two years before reaching agreement, and it was not until 1937, at the Machynlleth Eisteddfod, that the old Eisteddfod Council and the Gorsedd were brought together under a new constitution to form *Cyngor yr Eisteddfod Genedlaethol* (The Council of the National Eisteddfod).

Despite the reorganization, many of the problems of the Eisteddfod remained. Its economic situation had hardly recovered from the First War when it had to face the depression that followed the General Strike, which lasted throughout the thirties and made it difficult for venues to be found. As Professor Gruffydd pointed out, whereas earlier 'Aberdare and Caerphilly and Cardiff were falling over each other to embrace it, by today they are like people keeping a poor relation at arm's length.' Even so, an offer to provide a home for the Eisteddfod in 1934 came from Neath.

At the Caernarfon Eisteddfod in 1935 the attendance figures were unusually low, and one of the reasons given for this was the depression in South Wales. Gruffydd complained that the Eisteddfod was becoming 'more un-Welsh' ('yn fwy anghymreig') and backed his assertion by reporting that one of the stage conductors at Caernarfon had apologised for speaking English on the stage 'because many of the Welsh people present did not understand Welsh.'

The Chair at Caernarfon was won by a young student, studying at the University College of Wales at Aberystwyth, E. Gwyndaf Evans (Gwyndaf), for an *awdl* to *Magdalen,* and the Crown for a poem to *Ynys Enlli* was awarded to Gwilym R. Jones.

The Eisteddfod came to Pembrokeshire for the first time in 1936, when it was held at Fishguard. It was opened on the Monday morning by the Lord Lieutenant, Sir Evan D. Jones, Bart., supported by the Member of Parliament for the county, Major Gwilym Lloyd George, Eisteddfod officials and local dignitaries. On the Tuesday morning, before eight o'clock, the Gorsedd procession assembled on Fishguard Square and, led by the mounted figure of Sieffre o Gyfarthfa (Captain Geoffrey Crawshay), the Herald Bard, proceeded to the Gorsedd Circle erected on Penslade, overlooking Fishguard Bay. At this ceremony, J. J. Williams (J.J.), the winner of the Chair at Caernarfon in 1906 for his *awdl* to *Y Lloer* (The

Moon), and at Llangollen in 1908 for a poem in memory of *Ceiriog*, was installed Archdruid in the place of Gwili (J. Gwili Jenkins: 1872-1936) who had died the previous May. Gwili, a native of Hendy near Pontardulais, had achieved distinction as a theologian and had become professor of New Testament Exegesis at the University College of North Wales, Bangor. He was awarded the Crown at Merthyr Tydfil in 1901 for a *pryddest* to *Tywysog Tangnefedd* (The Prince of Peace), and had been archdruid since 1932.

The programme of the day at Fishguard contained an explanatory note on the procedure to be followed during the crowning ceremony:

> The Ceremony of Crowning the Bard will be according to the rites of the Bards of the Isle of Britain. He will be proclaimed by sound of Trumpet; the Gorsedd Recorder will call the Muster of the Bards; the Adjudication will be delivered; the successful Bard will be escorted to the platform by two of the Principal Bards. The Victor will be duly invested as Crowned Bard of the National Eisteddfod of 1936. The Bards will deliver their addresses, and Madam Margaret Thomas will sing the Crowning Song. The whole ceremony will be under the direction of the Gorsedd of Bards.
>
> SPECIAL NOTICE. No person whatsoever other than
> (a) Members of the Gorsedd in their Official Robes;
> or
> (b) Official Representatives of the Eisteddfod Committee in the capacity of Adjudicator, or otherwise officially engaged in the Ceremony of Investiture, can be allowed to take part in the Ceremony of Crowning the Bard on the Eisteddfod Platform. The whole of these proceedings will be under the sole control of the Gorsedd, exercised through the Recorder, and the Herald Bard as Master of the Ceremonies.

Opposition to the increasing anglicisation of the Eisteddfod reached a climax at the Machynlleth Eisteddfod in 1937 when several of the adjudicators, including Professor W. J. Gruffydd, Dr Iorwerth Peate, Dr Thomas Parry and Miss Cassie Davies, resigned in protest against the appointment of the Marquess of Londonderry, who had local connections, as president of the day.

Peate had already written in *Heddiw*, the lively journal founded by Aneirin Talfan Davies in 1936, that the Eisteddfod would have to choose between holding the festival in the large cities and towns, where it would have to fight against having the English on the local committee, or in the small country towns, where it would have to be on guard against the anglo-maniacs.

It had long been felt that insufficient regard was being paid to the prose competitions and that the limelight was wholly directed on the poets. There had been suggestions that the Crown should be awarded as a prize for prose, reserving the Chair for poetry, and other proposals were put forward from time to time in an effort to provide a rightful place for prose in the Eisteddfod programme. In 1937, a Gold Medal for Literature, to be awarded as the chief prize for prose writing, was presented by Sir Howell J. Williams. It was offered for a collection of essays at the Machynlleth Eisteddfod and was won by J. O. Williams, Bethesda, for his *Tua'r Gorllewin ac Ysgrifau Eraill*. The recipient wears the medal on a neck ribbon and is offered membership of the Gorsedd with the status of a *prifardd*.

In 1938 the Eisteddfod visited Cardiff for the first time since 1899 and it was feared that the growth of the city during the intervening years and its cosmopolitan nature would require the festival to be conducted largely in English. On the contrary, for the first time for a number of years, the literary competitions were conducted entirely in the Welsh language.

A significant event during the Cardiff Eisteddfod was the decision of the Honourable Society of Cymmrodorion to publish *Y Bywgraffiadur Cymreig* (The Dictionary of Welsh Biography) under the editorship of Dr R. T. Jenkins, with Sir J. E. Lloyd as consultant editor. At the same Eisteddfod, the National Union of Welsh Societies met to consider the legal position of the Welsh language in the courts. They decided to launch a petition demanding official recognition for the Welsh language in Welsh courts of law and in public life.

On the recommendation of the Literary and Music Committees of the Eisteddfod Council, substantial prizes were offered in the 1939 and 1940 Eisteddfodau for essays of a more comprehensive nature. A prize of £100 was offered, for example, for an essay on 'The Rise and Fall of the Welsh Language' and a period of three years allowed for the work to be completed.

The Council had in 1938 relinquished the tenancy of its offices in Chancery Lane, thus bringing to an end the Eisteddfod's long connection with London.

The Denbigh Eisteddfod of 1939 was the first to be held under the new constitution which had been adopted at Machynlleth. Hitherto, the National Eisteddfod had been, in effect, a local eisteddfod on a large scale organised by a local committee but under the new constitution it became the responsibility of a national body, the Council of the National Eisteddfod of Wales, which comprised the country's leading scholars in literature, music and the arts. The 1939 festival was significantly described as *Yr Eisteddfod Genedlaethol yn Ninbych* (the National Eisteddfod *in* Denbigh), as opposed to the previous designation of *Eisteddfod Genedlaethol Caerdydd* (The National Eisteddfod *of* Cardiff), signifying that it was the National Eisteddfod of Wales, which was being held at a place selected by the National Eisteddfod Council.

Denbigh had the unenviable distinction of being the first Eisteddfod at which both the Crown and the Chair were withheld. It was also the first Eisteddfod at which a Scottish choir competed. Although the Eisteddfod concluded officially on the Saturday, a *Gymanfa Ganu* was held in the pavilion on the Sunday evening in the presence of Princess Alice and the Earl of Athlone, and attended by a capacity audience.

With the outbreak of war, the Eisteddfod authorities realised that the festival proclaimed at Bridgend in 1939 could not be held there in 1940, and even if there had been any doubt on the matter, it was settled when the Government declared that area to be liable to air attack on account of its industrial nature. Under the circumstances, the Eisteddfod Council assumed responsibility for arranging an Eisteddfod, diminished in form but national in nature. The Council's first task was to find a venue and, with this end in view, it advanced £1,000 to the Council of Social Service for South Wales and Monmouthshire towards the purchase of a large pavilion seating 5,000 people at Mountain Ash on condition that it would be able to hold a National Eisteddfod there in August 1940 and, if need be, in the years following the war. The Eisteddfod was proclaimed at an official Gorsedd ceremony in Parcydyffryn, Mountain Ash, in May 1940. The rule under which the festival had to be proclaimed at least a year and a day in advance, in accordance with ancient usage, was waived for the duration of the war.

In July 1940, the Council was informed by the Government that Mountain Ash had by now been listed as an area which might be subject to enemy attack, therefore public gatherings would not be allowed. The Eisteddfod was barely a month away and all the arrangements had been finalized. The Emergency Committee appointed by the Council to handle unforeseen eventualities was soon put to the test. It approached the Welsh department of the BBC at Bangor for its advice and co-operation, and the idea of a broadcast Eisteddfod, variously referred to as the Radio Eisteddfod or the Eisteddfod of the Air, came into being. So it was that at the height of the war, the people of Wales and Welshmen abroad, (especially those in the armed forces), were able to enjoy the Eisteddfod in a truncated form, by courtesy of the BBC. Cynan recalls how he visited Cwm Croesor during Eisteddfod week and heard one of the broadcasts there, 'the radio set on the garden wall and the quiet, thoughtful denizens around it and hanging upon every word as though their own fates were in balance.'

Following the Eisteddfod of the Air, the Council made efforts to restore the festival to its traditional form, though on a reduced scale, and a three-day event was arranged in the local church hall at Old Colwyn in 1941. It suffered from the difficulties of war-time privations, but it benefitted from the fact that D. R. Hughes, now Joint-Secretary of the Eisteddfod Council with Cynan, resided at Colwyn Bay, and his presence largely accounted for the success of the Eisteddfod and for its completely Welsh character.

The Old Colwyn Eisteddfod raised a new hope in many hearts, for here the Welsh language was supreme and the feasibility of conducting the festival entirely through the medium of the Welsh language was demonstrated. In its restricted form the Eisteddfod was predominantly devoted to poetry and literature, which had long been the ambition of Professor W. J. Gruffydd, but even so he was among the first to request the restoration of music.

Although the Eisteddfod was being held in a small hall seating less than 600 people, the dream of a pavilion was much in the promoters' mind and it was, perhaps, something of an act of faith that a special prize of £100 should be offered for the best plan of 'a pavilion for the National Eisteddfod of Wales with seating accommodation for 12,000 people.'

The silver chair offered for the best ode to *Hydref* (Autumn) and won by Rowland Jones (Rolant o Fôn), was a war-time measure rather than a resort to the medieval custom.

A deputation from Cardigan had appeared before the Eisteddfod Council at Cardiff in order to invite the Eisteddfod to that town in 1940, but the invitation had been declined in favour of Bridgend. Before the end of 1941, however, the Eisteddfod Council was approaching the town of Cardigan seeking an invitation for the 1942 Eisteddfod, after Carmarthen had felt unable to offer it a home owing to the war situation.

The Cardigan Eisteddfod, though still on a reduced scale, was extended to include a selection of music competitions. The chief choral competition, however, was confined to choirs of not more than 30 in number, and male voice choirs were limited to eight. The adjudicators had travelled the country in order to select the best three choirs in each competition, and these were invited to appear on the Eisteddfod platform. There was disappointment when it was learned that the Chair offered for a poem *Rhyfel* (War) or *Creiddylad* (Cordelia) had been withheld, but the Crown was awarded to Herman Jones for a *pryddest* on *Ebargofiant* (Oblivion) and the Prose Medal was won by Gwilym R. Jones for his short novel *Y Purdan* (Purgatory).

At the Cardigan Eisteddfod, a group of young men, many of whom were to become prominent lawyers, politicians and even Cabinet Ministers, formed themselves into an informal association which they called 'Group 42', for the purpose of discussing and formulating ideas that could be implemented when the war was over. Although the Group was short lived, it laid the groundwork for much of the post-war thinking in Wales, and it provided an example of the kind of ancilliary activity that is inspired from time to time by a chance discussion on the Eisteddfod field, or over a glass of ale at a hostelry, often late at night, during Eisteddfod week.

The Cardigan Eisteddfod is remembered by those who were present for the appearance of the young tenor, David Lloyd, and his rendering of the Welsh hymn, 'Mi glywaf dyner lais' (I hear a tender voice), following a speech by David Lloyd George, who now presided regularly on the Thursday of Eisteddfod week.

The wartime Eisteddfodau appeared to be destined to be held at places other than the chosen location. The 1940 Eisteddfod planned for Bridgend was moved to Mountain Ash, but was eventually broadcast from Bangor. Colwyn Bay was the site chosen for the 1941 Eisteddfod, but it had to be held at Old Colwyn. The Eisteddfod it was hoped would be held at Carmarthen in 1942, was staged at Cardigan. The Eisteddfod that should have been held at Llangefni in 1943 was moved to Bangor in response to an appeal by the Minister of Transport.

The Eisteddfod had been held at Bangor in 1874, 1890, 1902, 1915 and 1931, on expansive meadows or beside the Menai, but this time it came rather unexpectedly, and had to be housed in the local theatre and in neighbouring chapels.

In view of the government order restricting the use of metals and other materials there was no Chair or Crown offered and medals, designed by Sir William Goscombe John, were substituted as prizes. Dewi Emrys who received the medal for the Chair poem had already won the Chair at Liverpool (1929) and at Llanelli (1930), and may not have been as disappointed at the absence of a Chair as a first-time winner would have been. The medal for the Crown poem on *Rhosydd Moab* (The Moors of Moab), was awarded to Dafydd Owen, a student at Bala-Bangor Theological College and a 'pupil' of Dewi Emrys's weekly poetry column, *Y Babell Awen*, in *Y Cymro*.

The Bangor Committee broke new ground with a translation into the vernacular of Mendelssohn's 'Hymn of Praise', and also with the reception it gave to representatives of foreign countries — the deputy Prime Minister of Yugoslavia, the Secretary of Education from Belgium, and representatives of the governments of Czechoslovakia and the U.S.S.R. They were received on the Eisteddfod platform, following the chairing ceremony, by the Archdruid Crwys as 'emissaries from the countries of Europe visiting, for the first time since the days of Owain Glyndŵr, the court of the people of Wales.'

During the Bangor Eisteddfod a bilingual pamphlet, *Eisteddfod y Cymry* (The Eisteddfod of the Welsh), written by Dr Thomas Parry, with an English translation by Dr R. T. Jenkins, was published primarily in order to interest children in the Eisteddfod and to provide its historical background for them in convenient form, and it was widely distributed, free of charge, to schools in the locality in which the Eisteddfod was held.

An invitation to provide a venue for the 1944 Eisteddfod was received from Llandybïe, in Carmarthenshire. With the co-operation of the people of neighbouring villages, it was decided to launch a festival lasting a week, in place of the three-day event which had been held annually since the outbreak of war, and the Eisteddfod Council was able to relax its control and to share its powers with the local committee. Llandybïe thus provided an opportunity, and the occasion, for the Eisteddfod to re-establish itself in preparation for the post-war period. Alun Talfan Davies, vice-chairman of the Llandybïe Eisteddfod Committee, commented that, although it could not be claimed that sublime heights had been reached in any one of the arts at Llandybïe, it was 'a popular Eisteddfod — a colourful Gorsedd with five thousand people gathered around the stone circle — twenty thousand visiting the new Art Exhibition — the two halls that had been set aside for drama proving too small — and the field, the main platform of the Eisteddfod, seething with schemes for the future. It was all a mirror of the head and of the heart of Wales.'

The Llandybïe Eisteddfod was able to boast a handsome profit of £2,950, one half of which was handed to the Eisteddfod Council, thus reimbursing it for the losses it had sustained in staging the earlier war-time eisteddfodau. The local committee also made a donation of £1,000 from the balance, so as to provide an annual prize of £50 for an essay or dissertation on some aspect of Welsh life or culture.

The Eisteddfod was blessed with perfect weather, and the village hall, and the marquee erected beside it, were packed to overflowing throughout the week. It opened on a high note on the Saturday evening, with an international concert in which representatives of many of the free countries of the world took part, including the Polish Army Choir and artists from Norway, France, Belgium, the Ukraine and the U.S.A. This notion of international cultural concord, begun at Bangor, was later developed through the vision and persistence of Harold Tudor, the British Council's Welsh Officer, and W. S. Gwynn Williams, the National Eisteddfod's Musical Director, until it became established in 1947 as the Llangollen International Music Eisteddfod.

The preparations for Rhosllannerchrugog Eisteddfod had been made while the war was still raging and had to be on a limited scale but with the cessation of hostilities in Europe these plans had to be changed rather rapidly. In place of the Miners' Institute, which had been generously loaned for the purpose, the Rhos Committee set about to provide a large pavilion that would accommodate the thousands now expected to attend the festival in a spirit of celebration and thanksgiving.

The Eisteddfod opened, however, with the stupefying news of the dropping of an atom bomb on the Japanese city of Hiroshima. People sensed that something strange and terrible had happened that day and some, at least, realised that they had witnessed the birth of a new era in the history of man.

Although hostilities were not yet over, the Rhos Eisteddfod is generally regarded as the first post-war Eisteddfod, and it was attended by a large number of men and women on leave or awaiting demobilisation from the forces. The Eisteddfod authorities arranged an official welcome for these people during the Thursday evening concert. Several hundred soldiers, sailors, airmen and nurses were assembled on the Eisteddfod platform, along with the band of the Welsh Guards, to receive their country's 'welcome home from the war', which was extended to them by the Archdruid Crwys, the Bishop of St Asaph and Alderman Emyr Williams, Chairman of the Eisteddfod Council. Two members of the forces were selected to respond to the welcome and David Lloyd, himself a Welsh Guardsman, and Tudor Evans, sang to the delight of the vast audience.

The second atom bomb had been dropped that Thursday

morning, on Nagasaki, and on the following day, just before noon, during the choral-speaking competition, word reached the Pavilion that the Japanese had asked for terms of surrender. The announcement, made from the Eisteddfod platform, was received by the great audience in complete silence, as the blind poet and former archdruid, Elfed, was led to a microphone. He raised his right hand and, proclaimed the wone word: 'Gweddïwn' (Let us pray). The stillness that followed his 'Amen' was only broken when he announced the hymn 'Cyfamod hedd, cyfamod cadarn Duw' (Covenant of peace, firm covenant of God), which has surely, never before or since, been sung with such joyous fervour and thanksgiving, the last quatrain being repeated time and again. In their exhultation, people caressed and kissed each other, and tears welled in the eyes of strong men. The war was over, after six weary years of suffering and hardship, of man's inhumanity to man. At long last the answer to the eternal question *A oes heddwch?* was, truly, *Heddwch!*

The Welsh Guards commemorated the occasion by presenting a handsome silver cup as the prize in the chief male voice choral competition, in memory of their comrades who had lost their lives in the two world wars. A similar trophy had been presented by the Royal Welch Fusiliers in 1939 for the second male voice competition. At Rhos, also, a sum of two hundred guineas was handed over by *Cymry'r Dwyrain Canol,* Welsh men and women who had served with the armed forces in the Middle East during the war, to provide a prize to be awarded annually in the literary section.

Professor W. J. Gruffydd, for so long a critic of the Eisteddfod, was appointed its President in succession to the late Earl Lloyd George of Dwyfor.

The Rhos Eisteddfod realised a profit of £4,000, which it shared with the Eisteddfod Council. This principle of co-operation and joint responsibility as between the Council and the local committee, begun at Llandybïe, was adopted as the pattern for the future organization of the Eisteddfod and was reiterated in *Cyfarwyddion i'r Pwyllgor Lleol* (Guidelines for the Local Committee), which laid down that co-operation between the Local Committee and the Eisteddfod Council was essential.

The booklet *Eisteddfod y Cymry,* by Thomas Parry and R. T. Jenkins, was now expanded to include a section on *Gorsedd y Beirdd,* written by Cynan.

At the invitation of the French government the Eisteddfod Council sent a deputation to France in 1946 to investigate the status of the Breton language in education and community life in

Brittany. They were given every facility to interview the leaders of the Breton movement and Bretons of all shades of political opinion, and their findings were issued in a document published in Welsh, English, Breton and French.

The Eisteddfod was held at Mountain Ash in 1946 as the Eisteddfod Council, in collaboration with the Council of Social Service for South Wales and Monmouthshire, had secured the use of the Mountain Ash Pavilion at the beginning of the war. The festival received the support of the people of the Cynon valley, from Abercynon to Aberdare, which contributed substantially towards its success and to the realisation of a record profit of £9,000.

Princess Elizabeth attended the Eisteddfod at Mountain Ash and, within the Gorsedd circle at Dyffryn Park, she was initiated into the Gorsedd of Bards of the Isle of Britain, wearing the green robe of the novitiate. On account of the shortage of materials, the Princess had provided a length of white silk, which had been suitably dyed and made up by a Court dressmaker. She placed her hands between those of the Archdruid Crwys, who received her into the Gorsedd as an Honorary Ovate under the bardic title *Elisabeth o Windsor*.

Crwys was appointed Archdruid in 1939 and no one could have been better suited to hold the office during the war years. His unpretentious manner was suited to the austerity of the war-time ceremonies and his ready wit and jocularity provided a much-appreciated relief from the prevailing gloom. He was succeeded by Wil Ifan (the Rev. William Evans) the winner of the Crown at Abergavenny (1913), Birkenhead (1917) and Pwllheli (1925), who was installed at the proclamation ceremony of the Colwyn Bay Eisteddfod in 1947.

Colwyn Bay was a fitting place to pay tribute to D. R. Hughes upon his retirement as Joint-Secretary of the Eisteddfod Council. A resolution recording the Eisteddfod's debt to him was carried with acclamation at the annual meeting, and he was granted the highest available honour by being elected a Vice-president for life. He was succeeded by Ernest Roberts, who had been Secretary of the Bangor Eisteddfod in 1943.

The Eisteddfod continued to receive donations, trophies and prizes each year, along with bequests and commemorative trusts. When the Rt. Hon. D. R. Grenfell received a gift of a thousand guineas to mark the completion of 25 years' service as Member of Parliament for Gower, he handed it to the Eisteddfod Council in order to establish an annual prize in memory of his wife to be known as 'The Beatrice Grenfell Prize'. This prize was to be awarded for an essay on a subject reflecting the effect of industry on the life of Wales.

The awareness of a new spirit of co-operation and the sharing of responsibilities made it a more attractive proposition to invite the festival, and invitations from four towns in North Wales anxious to receive the 1949 Eisteddfod were considered by the Eisteddfod Council at Colwyn Bay. These were presented by deputations from Hawarden, Pwllheli, Dolgellau and Ruthin. Dolgellau was selected.

Gorsedd y Beirdd received with great regret the resignation, owing to indisposition, of Sieffre o Gyfarthfa (Captain Geoffrey Crawshay), who had been the Herald Bard since 1926. Captain Crawshay presented a handsome staff of office decorated with oak leaves and mistletoe, executed by Frank Roper, A.R.C.A., of the Cardiff School of Art, for use by his successors. He was succeeded by Captain R. W. Jones (Erfyl Fychan).

The difficulties in providing a building of sizeable proportions in which to hold the Eisteddfod reached a climax at Bridgend in 1948. The local organisers had to engage the services of no less than eight separate firms in order to erect a pavilion, which eventually cost £25,000. The Eisteddfod Council set up a Pavilion Committee to investigate the problem.

The award of the Chair at Bridgend caused a considerable stir. Hitherto, there had been no limit to the number of times that the Chair or the Crown could be won, except that since the Chair had been awarded to Dyfed for the fourth time at Merthyr Tydfil in 1901, there was a general feeling that no one should seek to win either on more than three occasions. Cadfan, Crwys, Cynan, Wil Ifan, Caradog Prichard and J. M. Edwards had each won the Crown on three occasions and J. T. Job had won the Chair three times and the Crown once.

The Chaired Bard at Bridgend was Dewi Emrys, who had been awarded the Chair at Liverpool (1929), Llanelli (1930) and Bangor (1943), and who had also won the Crown at Swansea in 1926. He was aware that an attempt to win further honours would incur the displeasure of the authorities but he assumed the Chair with evident pride and a visible defiance.

The Crown and the Chair competitions had always been regarded as incentives for young poets rather than ultimate goals. In the words of the poet R. Williams Parry, a Crowned or Chaired poet should go 'from his reward to his labour' and it was generally agreed that there was little purpose in the same poet being Chaired or Crowned time and time again which, in any case, discouraged aspiring poets. It was therefore decided that, henceforth, no one should be entitled to receive the Crown or the Chair more than twice.

At the Dolgellau Eisteddfod in 1949, R. Gwilym Roberts of Buenos Aires was selected to act as leader of the Welsh exiles attending the festival, and to respond on their behalf. To mark the occasion he presented a badge carved in ivory, the work of the artist R. L. Gapper, to the Eisteddfod. This badge was to be worn on a chain by the leader of the Welsh exiles at the ceremony of welcome each year.

The number of presidents was reduced from three each day to one, as there was no longer time for three speeches to be delivered daily, and it was also felt that it would be regarded as a more signal mark of honour to be invited to be President of the Day.

The first issue of *Corn Gwlad*, the new annual journal of Gorsedd y Beirdd and the Eisteddfod, appeared in 1949 under the editorship of John Eilian, the Crowned Bard of the Dolgellau Eisteddfod. It was hailed as 'a dignified, attractive and lively journal that would be a permanent link between an enlightened people and its national festival' but, regrettably, it ceased after the first issue.

The Dolgellau Eisteddfod claimed to have been 'the most Welsh' ever held: a Welsh translation was provided for every musical work so that all competitions were conducted in the Welsh language. The critics who maintained that this policy would exclude non-Welsh choirs and would spell the early demise of the Eisteddfod were soon silenced when it was announced that the first and second prizes in the Ladies' Choir competition had been won respectively by Plymouth and Blackpool.

The local committee took care to make available at Dolgellau a more dignified *Pabell Lên* (Literature Pavilion) than had been provided hitherto. It was officially opened by Bob Owen, Croesor, and a special session was arranged for the adjudication of the *awdl* to be delivered in its totality, which proved to be one of the most popular and significant features of the 1949 festival.

The Dolgellau pavilion, which was erected at a cost of £20,000, was equipped with a new type of sound amplification, based on that perfected for the Olympic Games held in London in 1948.

The Gorsedd decided to arrange regular exchange visits with its daughter-Gorseddau in Brittany and Cornwall, and with the *Oireachtas* in Ireland, and representatives of these institutions were welcomed by the Archdruid, Wil Ifan, at Dolgellau.

A strong deputation from the Gorsedd attended a joint-Gorsedd of Welsh, Breton and Cornish Bards at Tregastel in Brittany in April 1950, and it was considered that the visit had been beneficial to the Breton cause in general and that it had established *Gorsedd Llydaw* in the eyes of the authorities. Representatives of *Gorsedd y Beirdd* also visited *Gorseth Kernow*, in Cornwall, and the *Oireachtas* in Dublin.

The Caerffili Eisteddfod received unusual publicity as it was the first to implement the 'all Welsh rule'. All the competitions were conducted in the Welsh language, including the music competitions, which was no small achievement in an area that was largely anglicised. The rule was broken, however, by two speeches made from the platform. The Lord Mayor of Cardiff inadvertently did so when he extended a welcome to the overseas visitors, but the Member of Parliament for Caerffili, Mr Ness Edwards, took advantage of the occasion to deliver an attack on the Eisteddfod Council's language policy. Nevertheless, the principle that Welsh was the official language of the Eisteddfod was firmly established at Caerffili.

The provision of an adequate building to house the festival continued to be a problem and, during the preparations for the Caerffili Eisteddfod, consideration was given to the erection of a permanent pavilion based on plans, prepared by the Cardiff architect Howard Williams, which had been selected following a competition for a design for a purpose-built pavilion. However, an opportunity to rent a suitable building offered by Messrs. Woodhouse of Nottingham was accepted as a more economic proposition. The Council entered into a five year contract with this firm in 1950 to hire a structure of timber and corrugated iron, which continued to provide a roof for the Eisteddfod for the next quarter of a century.

The Local Government Act of 1948 had given local authorities powers to contribute up to sixpence in the £ towards cultural or leisure activities within their own boundaries but, even so, the right of the Caerffili Urban District Council to make a contribution under this Act was contested, and it became necessary to obtain counsel's opinion before a donation could be made.

Wil Ifan was succeeded as Archdruid by Cynan, who was installed at the Proclamation Ceremony held at Llanrwst on 15 June 1950. His place as Recorder was temporarily held by the Herald Bard, Erfyl Fychan.

Cynan led a delegation from *Gorsedd y Beirdd* to visit the Breton Gorsedd at Trehorenteuc in order to consolidate the *rapprochement* between the two Gorseddau, and found that the

Bretons were learning Welsh from a translation by the Grand Druid of Brittany, Eostig Sarzhau, of Caradar's 'Welsh Made Easy' under the Breton title *Cymraeg hep Poen* (Welsh without Pain).

The Llanrwst Eisteddfod coincided with the Festival of Britain and was featured as a part of that festival. Although important eisteddfodau, such as the Gwyneddigion Eisteddfod of 1791 and the Gwynedd Chair Eisteddfod, 1891, had been held at Llanrwst, it had never been the venue for the National Eisteddfod and there were some doubts as to whether such a small place could meet the expanding needs of the Eisteddfod, especially during the Festival of Britain year. As it turned out, Llanrwst received a record crowd for the Chairing ceremony when the Chair was awarded to Brinley Richards for his poem *Y Dyffryn* (The Valley). The Crown was won by T. Glynne Davies for a *pryddest* to *Adfeilion* (Ruins).

The new Constitution, which had taken so long to prepare, was presented to the annual meeting at the Aberystwyth Eisteddfod in 1952 by Sir David Hughes Parry, one of the Eisteddfod's legal advisers. It was fifteen years, he pointed out, since the merger between *Cymdeithas yr Eisteddfod* (the National Eisteddfod Society) and *Gorsedd y Beirdd* had taken place at Machynlleth, in 1937 and, from that date, the institution had been known as *Eisteddfod Genedlaethol Cymru* (The National Eisteddfod of Wales); its members were members of *Llys yr Eisteddfod* (the Eisteddfod Court) and its affairs were managed by the *Cyngor* (Council). There were provisions for the Council to honour a member who had rendered outstanding service to the Eisteddfod by electing him a *Cymrawd* (Fellow). The affairs of *Gorsedd y Beirdd* would be administered by *Bwrdd yr Orsedd* (the Gorsedd Board) appointed by Gorsedd members at their annual meeting.

The early fifties saw rapid progress in the arts and crafts at the Eisteddfod. The first steps were taken by the Caerffili Committee, which placed special emphasis on the fine arts and invited contemporary artists to exhibit their work under the patronage of the Eisteddfod instead of arranging competitions in the arts. The competitions were restored at Llanrwst but an important development took place there with the introduction of a Gold Medal for Art, the gift of J. R. Jones, Liverpool, which placed art on a par with poetry and literature in the Eisteddfod. The Medal is presented to the artist who exhibits work of outstanding quality and it was awarded at Llanrwst to Brenda Chamberlain for her 'Girl with a Siamese Cat'. The Llanrwst Committee provided a purpose-built pavilion to house the art and craft exhibition on the Eisteddfod field and the success of this provision was so immediate that the idea was adopted by the Eisteddfod Council in the following year, at Aberystwyth, as a permanent feature.

A further step in establishing the fine arts was the introduction of a Gold Medal for Architecture at the Ystradgynlais Eisteddfod, to be awarded to the architect or architects who had made the most significant contribution to architecture in Wales during the preceding year. The Medal was presented by Dr T. Alwyn Lloyd, but no one was considered worthy of it at Ystradgynlais.

The 1952 Eisteddfod had been proclaimed in the shadow of the ruined tower of Aberystwyth Castle on 20 June 1951, a setting that greatly pleased the Archdruid Cynan. By a special resolution of the Gorsedd, his tenure of office was extended by one year so that his successor would come into office as the new constitution came into force at the Rhyl Eisteddfod in 1953.

The Aberystwyth Committee provided an improved Literary Pavilion, a timber building on the Eisteddfod field, with a seating capacity for 500,.which proved to be far from adequate.

When it was first mooted that the North Wales seaside resort of Rhyl proposed inviting the Eisteddfod in 1953, there was considerable opposition to the idea of taking it to such an anglicised area, but it was soon realised that the hinterland had a solid tradition based on centuries of Welsh culture.

The Rhyl Committee was determined to give Drama its rightful place and had planned to engage the Pavilion Theatre, which had one of the finest stages in North Wales, but it was forestalled by a travelling circus and, consequently, the Committee committed itself to hiring the Queen's Theatre, thus providing the facilities of a professional theatre for Eisteddfod drama.

A memorable moment at the Rhyl Eisteddfod was the delivery of his presidential address in impeccable Welsh by the actor and dramatist Emlyn Williams, who informed his audience that he had submitted an entry in the drama competition at the Mold Eisteddfod in 1923, with a play on Owain Glyndŵr, but it had not been considered worthy of the prize of one hundred guineas!

The Eisteddfod platform at Rhyl was fitted with stage curtains, and a new system of sound amplification, based on that used in cinemas, was introduced. An exhibition of rural crafts and industries, with craftsmen following their skills in public view, proved so popular an innovation that it became a regular feature.

An effort had been made, at the Aberystwyth Eisteddfod, to bring new life to the Chief Choral contest by staging it on the Monday afternoon, and this was followed at Rhyl, but with little success as there were only two competitors. There was, however, a record number of entries for the Second Choral Competition, for mixed choirs of less than 80 voices.

On account of the traditional reticence of contestants, and the strict secrecy that necessarily surrounds the whole procedure, it is impossible to say how many women, if any, had ever competed for the Chair or the Crown. When Ernest Roberts and Cynan, the joint-secretaries, discovered that the Crown at Rhyl had been won, for the first time, by a woman, they were most anxious to keep the matter a complete secret. They conspired together and invented a rumour to mislead the news hounds to the effect that the winner had already won the Crown twice and was, therefore, ineligible to receive it. They released this story through an unwitting accomplice at Morris's bookshop in Caernarfon and, while the false trails were pursued, Dilys Cadwaladr was left in peace and able to bring an unexpected and pleasant surprise to the nation.

The Rhyl Eisteddfod was also memorable for a visit by Her Majesty the Queen, the first since her succession as her previous visit, to Mountain Ash in 1946, was as Princess Elizabeth.

The Ystradgynlais Eisteddfod of 1954 will surely rank as the wettest on record. It rained every day of that week, and the conversion of the field into a quagmire greatly inhibited social intercourse. The Gorsedd ceremonies had to be held in the local cinema, and the *Manchester Guardian* correspondent could not decide which was the most desolate sight 'a white-robed Druid under an umbrella, or a white-robed Druid looking as if he wished he had one.' The dismal scene was much relieved, however, by the performance of the floral dance on the Eisteddfod platform following the chairing ceremony.

Gorsedd y Beirdd, in particular, and Wales in general, mourned the death of the former Herald Bard, Captain Geoffrey Crawshay (Sieffre o Gyfarthfa), who had played a significant role in improving Gorsedd ceremonies. In his memory, the Captain Crawshay Memorial Fund presented two silver trumpets, which had sounded the fanfare at the Coronation of Her Majesty the Queen at Westminster Abbey, to the Gorsedd. Two members of the Llanrug Brass Band were appointed trumpeters in place of those from the Welsh Guards who had served in that capacity since the Dolgellau Eisteddfod.

Mrs W. M. Coombe-Tennant (Mam o Nedd), who had been appointed Mistress of the Robes in 1918, resigned from that office in 1954, and she was succeeded by Mrs Maude Thomas (Telynores Rhondda).

The weather at Pwllheli more than compensated for the deluge of Ystradgynlais, and the seaside setting was an additional attraction which led to the financial success of the 1955 Eisteddfod. Its cultural quality was also notable, and there were no less than thirty-six entries submitted in the Crown competition.

The Council had intended that D. R. Hughes should be the first to receive the honour of becoming a *Cymrawd* but he died before it could be conferred upon him, and the distinction then fell on Canon Maurice Jones (Meurig Prysor), former Principal of St David's College, Lampeter, who had served as a Treasurer of the Eisteddfod (1937-1955) and was also the first to hold the office of *Derwydd Gweinyddol,* the senior position open to a member of the Druidic Order who had not won a Chair or a Crown.

At the 1956 Eisteddfod, held at Aberdare, the Crown was offered for a metrical play, but none of the entries was considered worthy of the prize.

The problem of the pavilion continued to cause concern and, in 1956, a commission was set up to review the situation and to consider the feasibility of purchasing a permanent pavilion, but it recommended that the arrangement with Messrs. Woodhouse should continue.

Mrs Coombe-Tennant (Mam o Nedd) died in 1956 and left the Gorsedd a legacy of £5,000. The Gorsedd regalia was valued, for insurance purposes, at £4,140 : the most precious item was the Hirlas Horn which was estimated to be worth £2,000.

The Gorsedd Board issued a handbook for the guidance of local committees, indicating the procedure to follow in preparing for the Proclamation and Eisteddfod ceremonies. It also decreed that the Gorsedd symbol of 'the ineffable name' should appear without exception on the Crown and on the Chair offered at the National Eisteddfod each year, whatever their design.

At the Llangefni Eisteddfod in 1957, the Crown was again offered for a verse-play and, this time an entry worthy of the prize was found in Dyfnallt Morgan's *Rhwng Dau* (Between Two).

The rising costs of staging the Eisteddfod, and the consequent difficulties facing villages or small towns wishing to invite it, produced another Commission in 1957, set up to review the festival's finances and the recurring question of purchasing a permanent pavilion. The Eisteddfod that year was the first ever to show a profit of more than £10,000, and this despite the fact that Llangefni was one of the smallest towns in which it had been held. The local committee shared this profit with the Eisteddfod Council in the customary manner and, instead of dissipating its own half of the share by dividing it among the many worthy causes of the locality, it set up a fund with a trust to administer it, and used the yearly interest to promote the arts in Anglesey.

Ebbw Vale had made preparations extending over a period of twelve years to invite the Eisteddfod to the anglicised county of Monmouth. When the first invitation was extended, in 1948, it caused considerable surprise throughout Wales and few people questioned the Council's decision to accept Cardiff's invitation. Undaunted, Ebbw Vale applied again in 1956 and, on this occasion, the invitation was accepted and the Eisteddfod returned to Gwent after thirty years. The decision was more than justified by the success of the festival. There was an excellent attendance despite the fact that the Empire Games had been held at Cardiff only a fortnight earlier, and also in spite of bad weather for a good part of the week. But even those who admitted its success were inclined to doubt the wisdom of taking the festival to such an English-speaking area. 'What's left apart from the Gorsedd pillars?' asked one commentator, who answered his own question by pointing out that there remained a new understanding of, and sympathy for, things Welsh; and a realisation among the ordinary folk of Monmouth that they were the inheritors of a great Welsh patrimony.

The Eisteddfod Court, at its annual meeting at Ebbw Vale, sent a loyal message to the Queen expressing its joy at her decision to create her eldest son, Prince Charles, Prince of Wales. The Gorsedd Board sent its greetings to the Prince, together with a bound copy of the booklet *Hanes yr Eisteddfod* (the Story of the Eisteddfod). It also commissioned its Recorder, Cynan, to prepare a revised version of *Tywysog Gwlad y Bryniau*, a translation of 'God Bless the Prince of Wales', to be sung at the close of the chairing ceremony at Ebbw Vale.

The pavilion problem was urgently considered by the review commission, and also by a panel of experts set up by the Caernarfon Eisteddfod Committee, but they both came to the conclusion that there was no way of improving the existing arrangement and, accordingly, the contract with Messrs Woodhouse was renewed for a further term.

In 1953 the Welsh Office had issued a new flag for Wales upon which the traditional dragon was considerably reduced in size and encircled in a garter bearing the motto *Y ddraig goch ddyry cychwyn* (The red dragon gives the lead). Many Welshmen had a strong dislike for this new flag, not only because of its unattractive motif but also because they felt it supplanted the banner of the Red Dragon borne by Henry Tudor at Bosworth Field and, before him, by Cadwaladr, the seventh century prince of Gwynedd. Some also considered the motto laughable as it was a line taken from a supplicatory *cywydd* requesting the gift of a bull. The Gorsedd Board took an active part in this matter following a failure to receive an assurance from the Constable of Caernarfon Castle that the traditional flag would be flown from the Eagle Tower during the proclamation of the Caernarfon Eisteddfod in 1959. In the name of the Gorsedd of Bards, as custodians of the heraldic traditions of Wales, it declared that the banner of Cadwaladr was the true banner of Wales, and refused to acknowledge the badge device of 1953. It circularised all local authorities in Wales and made representations to the Secretary of State for Wales, Mr Henry Brooke, following which it was decreed by royal command that nothing but the traditional flag shall be flown in future as the official flag of Wales, and its unattractive supplanter was withdrawn.

Some thought had been given to holding the 1959 Eisteddfod in London to mark the Silver Jubilee of the Eisteddfod held at the Albert Hall in 1909, but a meeting of prominent London Welshmen held at the London University decided to reject the idea on the grounds that it might harm the work of the Welsh churches in London, and maintained that the Eisteddfod was an indigenous institution which should not be held outside Wales. Although the London Welsh Association dissented from these views, no invitation was received and the Eisteddfod went to Caernarfon.

The Proclamation Ceremony held at Caernarfon Castle was undoubtedly the most colourful and dignified ceremony held in that stronghold between the Investitures of 1911 and 1969. The proceedings were enlivened by the acrobatics and high pitched calls of a sociable chough that hovered over the harp and all but perched on the Archdruid's crown!

During the Caernarfon Eisteddfod, the Eisteddfod Council published its intention to establish a Pavilion Fund and transferred £14,000 from its general funds with the declared intention that the Fund should assist local committees to meet the increasing costs of staging the Eisteddfod each year. It also made an appeal to local authorities to subscribe up to one-tenth of a penny rate, as authorised by a Private Member's Bill promoted by Peter Thomas, Member of Parliament for Conway (and later Secretary of State for Wales): hitherto local authorities were only able to contribute to cultural and recreational facilities within their own areas, whereas under the new Act they were enabled to make a contribution to the local funds of the National Eisteddfod wherever it was held.

A proposal, that had first been put forward in 1893, to appoint a full-time officer to be responsible for the administration of the Eisteddfod's affairs, did not materialise until 1959 when it was decided to appoint two organisers, one for North Wales and the other for the South. John Roberts was appointed to the former post and T. D. Scourfield to the latter.

The extent to which steps were taken to conceal the identity of the successful poet, prior to the Chairing or Crowning ceremony, is illustrated by Brinli (Archdruid 1972-1975) in his book *Hamddena*. He and T. Llew Jones, the chaired bard of Ebbw Vale, had been invited to address congratulatory verses to the winner of the chair at Caernarfon. Although they met daily on the Eisteddfod field and freely discussed their joint assignment, Brinli was completely taken aback to find, a few minutes before the Chairing ceremony, that the Chair had been awarded to none other than T. Llew Jones himself, who had kept the secret even from his closest friends.

From time to time, the Eisteddfod, and *Gorsedd y Beirdd* in particular, were subjected to the castigation of newspaper critics. In 1959 a woman correspondent of the *Western Mail*, Jane Pugh, asked who was 'responsible for making the Archdruid look like a cross between a Pharaoh and a Roman Senator?' and speculated that 'the inspiration must have come from the painting of Dante's meeting with Beatrice on the Bridge.' She returned two days later to remind her readers that a slashing attack on Gorsedd untidiness had been made, some years before, by Professor Timothy Lewis, son-in-law of Beriah Gwynfe Evans, the Gorsedd Recorder from 1922 to 1927, and brother-in-law to Gwilym Rhug, who was Recorder from 1927 to 1931. Cynan, it was maintained, had been appointed Recorder in 1933 (in fact, he was appointed in 1935) with a mandate to tidy up the Gorsedd, and the Herald Bard, Captain Geoffrey Crawshay, had been mounted on horseback at the head of Gorsedd processions so as to be able to keep better control of the Gorseddigion. Before 1933, it was claimed, 'the Gorsedd had maintained its dignified dress. The Bards were all wearing dark lounge suits and black shoes with their robes, and as far as my memory serves me, the Archdruid alone wore laurel leaves. After 1933 the Gorsedd dress started to get fancier and fancier. Bits of gold lamé and lashings of laurel leaves arrived, and white shoes peeping out coyly from beneath the robes like friendly little white mice.'

The Gorsedd Banner had become frayed after over sixty years' use and its colours and gold embroidery had faded. In 1959 a new

Banner was made, to the exact design of the old, by Miss Iles of Brynsiencyn, and the cost of £100 was met by Señor Hywel Hughes of Bogota. Mrs A. M. Weeks (Cerddores Moelfre) was appointed Mistress of the Robes in succession to Mrs Maude Thomas (Telynores Rhondda).

At the Proclamation Ceremony of the Cardiff Eisteddfod, held within a stone cricle in the grounds of Cardiff Castle on 11 June 1959, Trefin (Edgar Phillips : 1889-1962) was installed Archdruid in succession to William Morris. Trefin had won the Chair at Wrexham in 1933 and he was regarded as one of the finest *cywydd* poets of this century. He had been Grand Sword-bearer since 1947 and he was succeeded in that post by the author.

Trefin presided over the Gorsedd ceremonies at Cardiff in 1960 wearing a new robe, presented by members of the London Welsh Association, and the old one, which had been in use since 1895, was deposited at the National Museum of Wales, along with an inscribed list of former Archdruids. Cardiff Castle provided a historic setting for the Gorsedd ceremony held on the Tuesday morning of Eisteddfod week, and the bardic procession brought colour and pageantry to the streets of the city, but by the Thursday morning the weather had changed to such an extent that the ceremony had to be held indoors, at the Reardon Smith Lecture Theatre.

At Cardiff, the Eisteddfod was honoured by a visit by the Queen and the Duke of Edinburgh, the Prince of Wales, Princess Anne, Princess Alexandra and Prince Michael of Kent. The royal party was greeted with a fanfare sounded by the Gorsedd trumpeters and the Queen and the Duke were escorted by T. W. Thomas (Ab Eos), the chairman of the local committee, to the Eisteddfod platform, where they were received by the Archdruid.

There were eight competitors for the Chair, offered for an *awdl*, either to *Morgannwg* (Glamorgan) or to *Dydd Barn* (Day of Judgement), but the adjudicators considered that none was worthy of the prize. The Herald Bard and the Grand Sword-bearer thereupon laid the Grand Sword across the Chair, carved of oak from the Llanofer estate, to indicate that the Chair of the Cardiff Eisteddfod had not found a deserving poet. On this royal occasion, however, the Queen was invited to occupy the Chair while she received an address of welcome, delivered in Welsh, by the President of the Eisteddfod Court, Sir Thomas Parry-Williams:

> We the Court of the National Eisteddfod of Wales, with its Council and Gorsedd, beg leave to offer Your Majesty our loyal thanks and greetings upon your most gracious visit to

the Eisteddfod. We recall with pleasure that as Princess Elizabeth you were graciously pleased to visit the National Eisteddfod in the year 1946 at Mountain Ash, and on that occasion you were invested as an Honorary Ovate of the Gorsedd of Bards with the title *Elisabeth o Windsor*. We humbly thank Your Majesty for continuing the tradition of Royal patronage for the National Eisteddfod of Wales from year to year and for graciously consenting to be present at the festival this year. We rejoice in the thought that your presence will enhance the dignity of this national institution, whose main objects are the fostering of the language and the promotion of the arts in Wales, the land whose name, we are proud to recall, is borne by Your Majesty's eldest son, His Royal Highness Prince Charles, Prince of Wales. We extend a most cordial welcome to His Royal Highness the Duke of Edinburgh who today will also be initiated Honorary Ovate of the Gorsedd of Bards and will take the title of *Philip Meirionnydd* ...We desire to express our loyal and dutiful attachment to Your Majesty's throne and person and it is our earnest hope that Divine Providence may long preserve you in health and strength to reign over your loyal subjects in peace and prosperity, and to promote the cause of culture throughout Your Majesty's realms.

The thunderous applause that followed the reading of the loyal address was indicative of the warmth of the welcome that greeted Her Majesty and served as a rejection of the attitude of seven members of the local committee who had resigned because they felt that the Queen's presence would break the all-Welsh rule.

This action was only one of a number of controversies that had afflicted the preparatory stages of the Cardiff Eisteddfod. There had been the usual objections to the extension of drinking hours, and an unexpected expostulation against the singing of a song from Vaughan Williams's *Sir John in Love* which included the chorus extolling 'Jolly good ale'. There was a dispute as to whether invitations to attend the Eisteddfod should be extended to Mr Henry Brooke and Lord Brecon, Secretary and Minister, respectively, for Welsh Affairs, on account of their role in the flooding of Tryweryn. Displeasure was expressed in certain quarters at the production of a satirical play called *Eisteddfa'r Gwatwarwyr* (The Seat of the Scornful), by Tom Richards, the plot of which related to the return of a Welsh girl from Paris with ideas of modernising Gorsedd fashions. The actual introduction of nylon robes for members of the Gorsedd provided a theme for the

Western Mail cartoonist, Geoffrey Evans, who portrayed two Bards walking in their robes in the rain, the one saying to the other: 'Fortunately, my tailor used drip-dry material this year!'

Prince Philip, Duke of Edinburgh and Earl of Merioneth, was initiated a member of the Gorsedd in the green robe of an ovate. He placed his right hand on the naked steel of the partly unsheathed Grand Sword, as a token of his patronage of the Gorsedd and the Eisteddfod, and was received by the Archdruid Trefin who said, in Welsh: 'I welcome you as a member of the Gorsedd of Bards of the Isle of Britain. May the grace of heaven surround you and all the members of the Royal Family.'

After considering the claims of the rival parties in Brittany, the Gorsedd recognised the leadership of Eostig Sarzhau, and the Breton Gorsedd was re-established by the Archdruid Trefin at a ceremony held at St Malo in 1961, at which Eostig Sarzhau was installed Grand Bard of Brittany.

Rhosllannerchrugog was the first place to which the Eisteddfod paid a second visit after the war. Following the appeal to local authorities under the provision of the 'Peter Thomas Act', which had realised £6,600, the Eisteddfod Council invited each County, Borough, Urban and Rural District Council in Wales to send representatives to the Rhos Eisteddfod in 1961. In response to this invitation, 220 Councillors and Council officials were received by the President, Sir Thomas Parry-Williams, at an official luncheon and were provided with seats in the pavilion so that they could have personal experience of the festival which their authorities had been asked to support. The practice has continued each year since that date, and has served to strengthen the connection between the Eisteddfod and local authorities.

Until 1961, the ceremony of welcome to Welshmen from overseas and the Literary Medal ceremony were both held on the Wednesday afternoon, and it was felt that one militated against the other. Accordingly, the Overseas Ceremony was moved to the Friday afternoon.

The *Western Mail* returned to its raillery on the opening day of the Rhos Eisteddfod with an article by John Lloyd, headed 'The Annual Market Place for Welsh Culture'. In it he described the National Eisteddfod as 'the most confused institution in a confused nation. Half circus and half concert, it has garnishings from chapel vestry, brains trust, school prize day, literary luncheon, sale of work and cocktail bar without cocktails. The word itself cannot be translated into an exact equivalent, which is fortunate for those who might be tempted to try ... Apart from the House of

Commons, no national assembly can ever have had so many critics and still flourish like a sprouting tree . . . Much of the criticism and animosity comes, understandably, from those unable to speak Welsh who accuse the Eisteddfod of locking the doors against them. But there remains a general ignorance of its aims, purpose and character.' In a subsequent issue, the editor observes that 'after the controversies that rocked last year's Eisteddfod (at Cardiff) the festival this year was bound to be comparatively serene. Even so, there have been the customary splutters of dispute. . . . In a country worried by Berlin, H-bombs, the space race and the common market, it is a striking thing that some people can still centre their main passions and anxieties in the preservation of the all-Welsh rule.'

It was estimated that more than 30,000 people had witnessed the proclamation of the National Eisteddfod at Llanelli on 21 June 1961. For the first time, the floral dance was accompanied by a troupe of instrumentalists consisting of two oboeists and four violinists, in addition to the usual harp accompaniment.

The Llanelli Eisteddfod had an air of sadness for those who were close to the Archdruid Trefin, for his health was visibly failing. An englyn which he had written lightheartedly in English some years earlier, and which he had entitled *Pruddglwyf* (Melancholy), came to mind:

> Where I pass the grass will grow, — and the wind
> Will wail in the willow;
> Unhallowed in a hollow,
> I will be laid well below.

He died at the end of August and his ashes were interred in the soil of his native Pembrokeshire.

Trefin was succeeded by Cynan, who thus became the first person ever to be re-elected to the office of Archdruid. Ab Eos (T. W. Thomas) was temporarily appointed Recorder in his place.

A Pavilion Appeal Fund was officially launched in 1963 with the object of raising £250,000, the interest from which would be used to assist local organising committees to meet the ever-increasing cost of preparing for the Eisteddfod, and not, as frequently assumed, for the purchase of a mobile pavilion. A panel of experts had demonstrated that it would not be prudent for the Eisteddfod Council to become the owner of such a building and, in particular, to be responsible for its maintenance and its removal from one end of Wales to the other each year. By the end of 1963, there was a credit balance of £32,640 in the Pavilion Fund.

The Llandudno Eisteddfod was disappointing because none of the eleven competitors who had submitted poems on the set subject, *Genesis*, was considered to be worthy of the Chair. Sir Thomas Parry-Williams, one of the adjudicators, described the level of competition as low and the Deputy Archdruid, William Morris, agreed with him. But Dr Thomas Parry, the third adjudicator, held the view that one of the entries, inspired by John Piper's great window in Coventry Cathedral, deserved the prize, although he confessed that he did not fully understand the poem. The Chair was therefore withheld, for the third time in a quarter of a century, and the Grand Sword was laid across its empty arms. The Archdruid Cynan strongly refuted allegations that an attempt had been made to persuade the adjudicators to change their decision so that the colourful chairing ceremony could take place.

A Gorsedd badge designed by the artist Douglas Williams and depicting the three shafts of light was introduced at the Llandudno Eisteddfod as a lapel badge.

The Llandudno festival was honoured by a visit by the Queen and the Duke of Edinburgh and there was much speculation as to whether Her Majesty would announce a date for the investiture of the Prince of Wales, particularly as she had, on the previous day, appointed Major Francis Jones to the office of Wales Herald Extraordinary, a title that had not been in use since the end of the fourteenth century.

The Eisteddfod's visit to Swansea coincided with a cricket match between the Australians and Glamorgan. This provided a rare opportunity for cricket-loving Eisteddfodwyr, (among whom was the octogenarian former Archdruid Crwys), to commute between St Helen's Ground and the Eisteddfod field.

An innovation at the Swansea Eisteddfod was the provision, in a small marquee, of a closed circuit television service which gave a simultaneous English translation of all that took place on the Eisteddfod platform. The service and the translation facilities were provided by Television Wales and the West Ltd., which also supplied hand receivers for those who wished to sit in the pavilion and obtain instant translation. By these means, the full compass of Eisteddfod activity was open to all, whether they were able to understand the Welsh language or not.

Mr Emrys Roberts was appointed Chairman of the Eisteddfod Council in 1964, in succession to Dr Haydn Williams, who had been chairman for the previous four years and whose untimely death was widely mourned.

The Gorsedd refused to exchange visits with the Breton Gorsedd in 1964 because the latter had consorted with representatives of an unacceptable organisation which called itself *Gorsedd Llundain* (The London Gorsedd).

The practice of awarding the main prizes for classical poems was criticized once more and it was contended that the two most colourful ceremonies of the Eisteddfod were being 'wasted on compiling poetry which the majority of Welsh people do not understand.' The Eisteddfod Council appointed a panel of leading poets and writers in 1965 to consider the relationship between poetry and prose in the Eisteddfod and to secure a rightful place for creative prose writing, equal to that granted to poetry.

The Council had already agreed to publish the winning entry in the Prose Gold Medal competition during Eisteddfod week, but there was a strong feeling, especially among prose-writers, that the ceremony bore poor comparison with the Crowning and Chairing ceremonies. Members of the panel agreed that it would not be feasible for the Crown to be awarded for the best prose work, as suggested by some, and it was therefore necessary to concentrate on improving the Prose Medal ceremony. The panel recommended that past winners of the Medal be invited to take part in the ceremony and that two of their number should conduct the Medal winner, suitably robed, to the platform where an appropriate song of greeting would be sung in his honour by a children's choir accompanied by a consort of harps. It also suggested that the ceremony should be in the hands of an experienced producer and that it should be known as *Seremoni'r Prif Lenor Rhyddiaith* (the Chief Prose Writer's Ceremony). The recommendations were accepted unanimously by the Eisteddfod Council and were implemented at the Port Talbot Eisteddfod in 1966.

The Gorsedd Board was disturbed to hear that certain records, including minutes of meetings held during the last century, had been sold to a collector of manuscripts in the United States of America and no one could account for their disappearance.

The centenary of the founding of the Welsh settlement in Patagonia was celebrated at the Newtown Eisteddfod in 1965, with a pageant, and a deputation from Patagonia was enthusiastically received at the Eisteddfod. A party of people from Wales flew to Patagonia to take part in the celebrations there, and included representatives of leading Welsh institutions, including the National Eisteddfod which was represented by its organiser for North Wales, John Roberts. The Eisteddfod Council gave a scholarship to Robin Gwyndaf Jones, of the Welsh Folk Museum, St Fagan's, to accompany the visiting party.

121

Cynan was succeeded as Archdruid in 1966, by Gwyndaf (the Rev. E. Gwyndaf Evans) who had won the chair, and was also runner-up for the crown, at the Caernarfon Eisteddfod of 1935 while he was still a student at the University College of Wales, Aberystwyth, and who was also widely known as an outstanding interpreter of the art of *penillion* singing.

In 1965 the Eisteddfod Council had recommended the Court to proceed with an application to secure a Royal Charter for the Eisteddfod in order that it should be incorporated on similar lines to the University, the National Museum and the National Library of Wales. The Court decided to defer its application for a Charter so as to obtain further information, and the Council appointed a panel, which included eminent lawyers, to prepare a report on the matter. The panel carefully weighed the arguments in favour, and against incorporation and, in a Memorandum, recommended that it be left to the Court to take a decision through the free vote of its members, but the Court, at its annual meeting during the Bala Eisteddfod, received the Memorandum without coming to a decision.

It had long been the custom for an appeal to be addressed each year to the sovereign seeking royal patronage for the Eisteddfod. At Aberafan, the Eisteddfod Court decided to petition the Queen for a permanent grant of favour, and this was given, in November 1966. The Eisteddfod Court was informed, next year at Bala, that the title *Eisteddfod Genedlaethol Frenhinol Cymru* (The Royal National Eisteddfod of Wales) was now secure for all time.

The Aberafan Eisteddfod will be remembered as *Eisteddfod y Cynhaeaf*. *Y Cynhaeaf* (The Harvest) was the subject of the *awdl*, for the Chair which was awarded to Dic Jones, a young farmer of Aberporth. His poem was described by one of the adjudicators as 'one of the best *awdlau* ever to emerge from an Eisteddfod competition ... truly a masterpiece.' There was an instant realization that a poem of high calibre comparable to R. Williams Parry's *Yr Haf* (1910) had been written, and all the volumes of the *Cyfansoddiadau a'r Beirniadaethau* (Compositions and Adjudications) were sold out within two days. For the first time the Crown, an intricate scrollwork mounted by a dragon, was not of silver but of stainless steel, symbolising the industry which had made Port Talbot world famous.

The Eisteddfod Council honoured Sir Thomas Parry-Williams, its retiring President, at the Bala Eisteddfod of 1967, by publishing a volume of his selected works as a tribute 'by more than one generation of his friends and students.' Cynan, the Recorder of the

Gorsedd and twice Archdruid, and Joint-secretary of the Eisteddfod Council since 1937, was elected President in his place.

The Herald Bard, Captain R. W. Jones (Erfyl Fychan), who had held office since 1947, tendered his resignation at Bala. He had acted as Recorder during Cynan's first term as Archdruid (1950-1954) and he continued to hold the office of Director of Gorsedd Examinations until his death early in 1968. Erfyl Fychan was succeeded as Herald Bard by the author, in whose place T. Gwynn Jones (Gwyn Tregarth) was elected Grand Sword Bearer.

The Eisteddfod also suffered the loss of its war-time Archdruid, Crwys, at the age of 93, and of its former legal adviser Dr William George (Llysor), on the eve of his 100th birthday.

The Crown, awarded at Bala for a poem on *Corlannau* (Penfolds), was won by Eluned Phillips (Eluned Teifi), the second woman to achieve this distinction and it was strongly rumoured that she was also the runner-up for the award.

In 1968, a festival was held to mark the quadringenary of the Eisteddfod held at Caerwys under a commission of Queen Elizabeth I. The Gorsedd of Bards took a leading part in the ceremony, which was attended by descendants of almost all the gentlemen named in the royal commission.

Over 6,000 entries were submitted in the 197 competitions at the Barry Eisteddfod in 1968, but 2,700 of these were in the Photography Sections. The Eisteddfod is memorable, however, for its concerts: the journal *Music and Musicians* commented that 'everything became unimportant beside the excellence of the evening concerts this year' and made special mention of the National Youth Orchestra and of the National Eisteddfod Choir at Barry, as 'the finest in living memory.'

For the first time for many years, the speeches of the Presidents of the Day were published in the annual report, including the brief address by Sir Cennydd Traherne, the Lord Lieutenant of Glamorgan, who had learnt Welsh and who reminded his audience that the Eisteddfod was the biggest festival of its kind in Europe, and the most powerful fortress in defence of the Welsh language.

The Gorsedd of Bards took an active part in the ceremony of the Investiture of His Royal Highness the Prince of Wales at Caernarfon Castle on 1 July 1969, at which it was represented by a delegation led by the Archdruid Tilsli. The Prince visited the Eisteddfod at Flint a month later.

Tilsli (the Rev. Gwilym R. Tilsley) had been installed Archdruid in succession to Gwyndaf at the proclamation of the

Ammanford Eisteddfod in June 1969. He had won the Chair at Caerffili in 1950 and also at Llangefni in 1957.

Some doubts were expressed as to the wisdom of taking the Eisteddfod to Flint, but the success of the festival far exceeded expectations, largely due to the industry of its chairman, Armon Ellis. The Eisteddfod Council gave consideration to the role of young people in the deliberations and administration of the Eisteddfod and appealed to the youth of Wales to become members of the Eisteddfod Court, and, during the Eisteddfod at Ammanford the following year, the President, Sir David Hughes-Parry, presided over a meeting at which young people were invited to express their own views on Eisteddfodic affairs.

The Ammanford Eisteddfod was the most financially rewarding ever to be held in South Wales with a profit of £20,000, which had only been exceeded at Bala, and attendances during the week were estimated at 200,000. Of the 182 local authorities in Wales, 152 had contributed to the Eisteddfod funds a total of £26,465.

The beginning of 1970 deprived the Eisteddfod of a number of its leading scholars and supporters, and among them the most prominent eisteddfodwr of the century, Cynan (Sir Cynan Evans-Jones). He had been Recorder of the Gorsedd of Bards for 35 years and Joint-secretary of the Eisteddfod Council for almost as long. He was the only person ever to be twice Archdruid, and he had been President of the Eisteddfod Court since 1967. Cynan gave to the Gorsedd a new dimension in the structure of the National Eisteddfod and he was the architect, with Captain Geoffrey Crawshay, of the colourful pageantry which characterises the ceremonies today. He was the most influential figure in this field since Iolo Morganwg himself.

Gwyndaf (the Rev. Gwyndaf Evans), the Chaired Bard of the Caernarfon Eisteddfod of 1935 and former Archdruid (1966-68), was appointed Recorder to succeed Cynan.

Before the annual meeting of the Gorsedd at Ammanford had terminated it received news of the sudden death, at a house nearby, of Alun Ogwen, the Membership Secretary of the Eisteddfod and chief steward of the Gorsedd. He was succeeded as Membership Secretary by D. Hugh Thomas.

At the Bangor Eisteddfod in 1971, Ernest Roberts retired after a period of service of 27 years, firstly as assistant honorary secretary of the Eisteddfod and, later, as joint-secretary with Cynan. R. T. D. Williams, then Clerk of the Montgomeryshire County Council, was appointed Secretary to the Eisteddfod Court. The Eisteddfod also lost its organiser for South Wales, T. D. Scourfield, on his appointment as secretary of the West Wales Association of the Arts, and J. Idris Evans was appointed in his place.

The governing body of the Gorsedd, *Bwrdd yr Orsedd*, gave much attention during 1971 to proposals put forward by Euros (the Rev. Euros Bowen) to modify the Gorsedd ceremonies so as 'to relate them more closely to the aims of the Eisteddfod, namely the fostering of the Welsh language, and the promotion of culture and the arts in Wales,' and the ceremonies were amended, both within the stone circle and on the Eisteddfod platform, at the Pembrokeshire Eisteddfod held at Haverfordwest in 1972.

The Bangor Eisteddfod was held in the grounds of Penrhyn Castle, where ordinary folks had never feasted in the past. Here Guto'r Glyn and Rhys Goch Eryri had once sung the praises of the lords of Penrhyn, who had made their fortunes from the nearby slate quarries. In his presidential address on the Thursday of Eisteddfod week, Ernest Roberts pointed out that the praises of the quarryman would be sung that day by poets competing for the Chair awarded for the best poem Y *Chwarelwr* (The Quarryman), and which would be adjudicated by three former Chaired Bards, the Rev. William Morris, Gwilym R. Jones and Dr. Thomas Parry, all three the sons of quarrymen.

During the ceremony of greeting the Welsh from overseas, a small boy appeared on the Eisteddfod platform and walked, carrying one of his sandals, towards the tall figure of the President Sir David Hughes-Parry, who was conveying the welcome of the huge assembly that packed the pavilion to the exiles. He offered his sandal to Sir David and clung passionately to his trousered leg. The child turned out to be Taro Nagashima, the two-year old son of a Japanese father and Welsh mother living in Tokyo.

In September 1971 the Archdruid Tilsli and the Recorder Gwyndaf met the Grand Druid of Brittany and the Grand Bard of Cornwall at Carlyon Bay in an effort to settle the differences that had existed between *Gorsedd y Beirdd* and the Breton Gorsedd for the previous eighteen years, and which were in danger of contaminating the good relations between Wales and the Cornish Gorsedd. The following agreement was signed by the parties named therein:

> We, Tilsli Archdruid of Wales, Eostig Sarzhau Grand Druid of Brittany and Trevanyon Grand Bard of Cornwall, together with Gwyndaf Recorder of the Gorsedd of Bards and Former-Archdruid of Wales, in convocation on this the third day of September 1971 at Carlyon Bay, hereby reaffirm our personal

allegiance and that of our respective Gorseddau to the Celtic heritage that has brought us together.

We acknowledge:

1. The supreme authority of the Archdruid of the Gorsedd of the Isle of Britain in all matters of Gorseddau constitution and practice.
2. The absolute necessity of guarding our respective gatherings against intrusion by alien and non-Celtic elements and personnel.
3. The complete autonomy of the Gorseddau of Wales, Brittany and Cornwall in their own domestic affairs.

The meeting coincided with *Gorseth Kernow* (the Cornish Gorsedd) held within the Circle of the Merry Maidens, an Iron Age stone circle, near Land's End.

The Breton Gorsedd owed its origins largely to the Welsh antiquary Carnhuanawc (Thomas Price : 1787-1848) who had followed the provincial eisteddfodau and had won a prize at the Welshpool Eisteddfod of 1824 for an essay on early relationships between the Armoricans and the Britons. His interest in Celtic antiquities grew as he travelled widely through the Celtic countries. He learned to speak Breton and, in urging close cultural ties between the Bretons and the Welsh, suggested that steps be taken to arrange an Eisteddfod in Brittany. Apart from the visit of the Vicomte de la Villemarqué to the Abergavenny Eisteddfod of 1838, there had been little contact between the two Celtic peoples until 1899, when a Breton delegation visited the Cardiff Eisteddfod, and the Gorsedd of the Bards of Brittany was established. Breton delegations attended most Eisteddfodau, and representatives of *Gorsedd y Beirdd* visited Brittany regularly until the outbreak of war in 1939. These visits were resumed after the war and the Eisteddfod Council took the initiative in investigating the complaints of the Bretons against the French government, but relationships later became strained and the exchanges ceased. It was hoped that the Carlyon Bay agreement would re-establish the close harmony of former years.

The National Eisteddfod had been to Pembrokeshire only once in its long history, when it visited Fishguard in 1936, and although that event was well remembered as one of the most successful of the century, there had been no subsequent invitation to the county. There had certainly been no thought of inviting it to visit Little England beyond Wales, as the southern half of the county had been known for centuries, and when a suggestion was made in the early sixties that the festival should be invited to Haverfordwest, it found little support. There were still considerable doubts when an invitation was eventualy extended in 1968. This was declined in favour of Ammanford but, two years later the invitation was renewed, and accepted. Even then many people questioned the wisdom of bringing the Eisteddfod to a town that had been basically devoid of a Welsh cultural tradition for over a thousand years. Haverfordwest, however, was the county town and a border town between Little England and the Welshery in the north, and the Eisteddfod would, in any case, be *Eisteddfod Sir Benfro,* able to draw support from all parts of the county. That this was the case was exemplified by Gwilym R. Jones, in his editorial in *Y Faner,* where he observed that the venture had 'proved that there was a way of wooing the non-Welsh speaking in Wales to the national fold and of bringing them close to the idea of one nation and that a bilingual one. To win over, by enlightenment and persuasion and by making Welshness more attractive, should be the aim of all those who value the Welsh way of life.'

The Proclamation Ceremony was held on 19 June 1971 within a stone circle erected on the Bridge Meadow, on the banks of the Western Cleddau and adjoining the town's soccer football ground. It was witnessed by a great concourse of people and the civic procession was one of the most impressive ever witnessed, largely on account of the unprecedented number of schoolchildren that took part in it.

Eisteddfod Sir Benfro, when it came, received the unstinted support of the county of Pembroke as a whole, despite the fact that only two out of every ten of its inhabitants were Welsh-speaking. Although the Eisteddfod coincided with the busiest week of the holiday season, in an area that relies largely on tourism, accommodation was found for all the thousands of eisteddfodwyr who flocked into the county town. Despite the additional difficulties caused by the postal strike and the miners' strike, and arguments over the structural stability of the pavilion, all the arrangements were concluded satisfactorily.

The number of entries in several of the competitions was disappointingly low, and the standard in others was such that awards were withheld, but the four major prizes for literature — the Chair, Crown, Prose Medal and Drama Prize — were all awarded for the first time since the Bala Eisteddfod, in 1967. It was remarkable too, in that the Crowned Bard, Dafydd Rowlands, performed the unique feat of also being the winner of the Literary Medal.

The provision of a special pavilion for people learning to speak the Welsh language was a much appreciated innovation, and the Eisteddfod Council also arranged a special welcome ceremony for them, and another to congratulate *Urdd Gobaith Cymru* (the Welsh League of Youth) on the celebration of its golden jubilee.

The Eisteddfod's role as a rallying point for Welsh movements was illustrated by the demands for suitable accommodation on the Eisteddfod field by no fewer than twenty-two organizations wishing to hold their annual meetings, or some form of gathering, in *Pabell y Cymdeithasau,* the pavilion specially provided each year for such meetings. Other organisations had to meet in the Literary Pavilion, or else in premises in the town. The Eisteddfod field was occupied by a record number of two hundred and five stands hired, in the main, by Welsh societies and booksellers.

Not only did all the local authorities in the county contribute financially towards the costs of the Eisteddfod, but they did so handsomely and gave a record total of £33,500, compared with £12,400 from all the local authorities in the rest of Wales. In addition, the people of the county raised £30,000. The cost of staging the festival amounted to £143,000, the highest ever, but even so the Pembrokeshire Committee was able to show a profit of £21,000, which it handed to the Eisteddfod Council.

While the 1972 Eisteddfod was a considerable success as a festival, it was attended by features which marred its popularity with local people, who had looked forward to a feast of poetry, song and goodwill. A contributor to *Y Genhinen,* in October 1972, expressed the view that 'it was a major venture on the part of the staunch Welshmen of Pembrokeshire to take the Eisteddfod among the "down belows", a greater venture than taking it to London or Liverpool ... My first impression on reaching Haverfordwest on Sunday was that the townspeople looked, with some fear and trepidation on this strange and alien monster that was coming to their midst, and their fears were confirmed on the Sunday evening by the behaviour of some of our young people ... Others had smashed signs, both in and off the field, and it is difficult to believe that this had in any way benefitted the cause of our language — in South Pembrokeshire anyway.'

He concluded that, 'on the whole, it was an Eisteddfod much like any other Eisteddfod. Perhaps it will be remembered as the Eisteddfod where the Crowned Bard also won the Literary Medal, or the Eisteddfod where the prize for the englyn was withheld, or the Eisteddfod where a Pavilion for Learners appeared for the first time, or perhaps the Eisteddfod where the Council (blessings upon them!) ruled that all notices on the field shall henceforth be in Welsh.'

During the Eisteddfod week, through the mediation of Alun Talfan Davies, staffs of office for use by Gorsedd stewards specially made by Alcoa Ltd., of Gorseinon, were presented to the Gorsedd of Bards. The staffs were made of aluminium, coloured white, blue, green and purple, and each staff bore a hand-tooled head, designed by the Herald Bard to symbolise 'the sign of the ineffable name'.

The Eisteddfod Finance Committee, at a meeting held at Shrewsbury in September 1972, considered in depth the rising costs of staging the festival. The overall cost had doubled in five years, although the cost of hiring the Pavilion and ancillary items had only increased from £30,000 to £42,000. The Committee firmly eschewed any notion of forming a company to share responsibility with the contractors and decided to renew the agreement with Messrs Woodhouse of Nottingham which was due to terminate in 1974, on revised terms. Apart from minor changes in the agreement, the Committee was satisfied that the existing arrangements could not be bettered.

The Dyffryn Clwyd Eisteddfod was proclaimed amidst peacocks and roses in the grounds of the red castle of Ruthin, in the heart of a countryside, on beholding which an English traveller once threw his hat in the air and shouted: 'Well done, God!'

At the proclamation ceremony Brinley Richards (Brinli), the winner of the chair at Llanrwst in 1951, was installed Archdruid to succeed Tilsli. Brinli, a native of Nant-y-ffyllon, had been an Honorary Legal Adviser to the Eisteddfod for a number of years and he was proud to announce that he was the first of his profession to be appointed Archdruid.

The Ruthin Eisteddfod was held on low lying meadows below the castle, beside a meandering stream. This was a pleasant setting for all purposes, except that when the heavy rains, that not infrequently characterise the first week of August, came on the Monday morning, the meadows bid fair to rival Noah's flood.

The highlight of the Ruthin Eisteddfod was reached when, for the first time for fifty-eight years, the Chair and the Crown were won by the same person. Alan Lloyd Roberts (Alan Llwyd), of Abersoch, was the first to repeat the achievement of Sir Thomas Parry-Williams at Bangor in 1915, and previously at Wrexham in 1912.

The local committee gave special thought to the provision of more dignified ceremonies for the presentation of the Literary

Medal and the Drama Award, with satisfying results, and it made special provision for Welsh language learners and arranged a tea party for them.

The Eisteddfod Court appointed Professor Idris Foster of Jesus College, Oxford, to succeed Sir David Hughes-Parry as President. Sir David was the architect of the Eisteddfod's constitution and his vast legal knowledge had been at the disposal of the authorities for nearly forty years. He had been President since 1970 and had died during his term of office in January 1973.

At the instigation of its Recorder, Gwyndaf, and with the collaboration of the Eisteddfod Finance Committee, the Gorsedd of Bards launched an appeal to raise £1,000,000 so as to ensure the financial structure of future Eisteddfodau by employing the interest on the capital to assist local committees.

In 1973, W. S. Gwynn Williams (Gwynn o'r Llan) completed fifty years as Director of Music of the Gorsedd and twenty years as chairman of the Eisteddfod Music Committee.

Undeb y Cymry ar Wasgar (the Union of the Welsh in Exile) celebrated its twenty-fifth anniversary in 1973 and, in the following year, an appeal was made for £10,000 to appoint a full-time officer to administer a new organisation to be known as 'Wales International'.

On the proposal of the Rev. Trebor Lloyd Evans, the Council set up a Commission in 1973 to consider the size and character of the Eisteddfod, and the manner in which it could best serve its purpose to promote the Welsh language and Welsh culture. The Commission considered aspects dealing with the Pavilion, the Eisteddfod field, the feasibility of a fixed or limited location, the procedure for inviting the festival and deciding on the venue, the constitution of the Eisteddfod Court, Council and Committees and their relationship with the local committees, the need for a central office and for an administrator, the situation of officers and of honorary officers, and the general organisation of the festival.

At the Ruthin Eisteddfod 1,155 people were interviewed on the Eisteddfod field, 60 per cent of whom declared that they followed the Eisteddfod regularly every year, and 30 per cent did so every other year. When asked whether they favoured a more static arrangement, 71 per cent stated that they wanted the present system to be retained, while 10 per cent expressed the view that the festival should make a circuit based on eight fixed locations. The Commission came to the conclusion that any limitation on location would fundamentally change the nature of the Eisteddfod.

The Eisteddfod Council considered the Commission's report in November 1974 and adopted its recommendations:

to establish a panel of experts to consider each year the layout of the site and pavilion in consultation with the local committee;

to retain the system of holding the Eisteddfod in North and South Wales in alternate years;

to select a venue three years, instead of two years, in advance of the date of the festival;

to reduce the number of Council members;

to establish an Executive Committee to deal with day-to-day matters, and to set up Panels in place of the existing Finance, Literary, Music, Drama, Publications, etc., Committees.

The question of establishing a central office with an overall administrator, which had been considered for a number of years, was further deferred.

With the continuing increase in the size and popularity of the Eisteddfod, there was a growing feeling that it was in danger of losing its original and primary purpose as a competitive meeting. There were those who felt that the Eisteddfod had become too massive altogether. Many of its followers were so heavily committed to meetings of societies and organizations held on the Eisteddfod field or in the vicinity, so as to coincide with the festival, that they had little time to enjoy the competitions in the Pavilion. The traditional gathering of bards in literary contest had developed into the focal point of the cultural life of the nation and, as such, it was necessary that it should be large and representative of all facets of Welsh life, and that it should be all-embracing and slightly disorderly. This view was expressed by T. D. Scourfield, formerly Eisteddfod organiser for South Wales, in an interview in *Y Genhinen* in 1973, in which he maintained that the conflicting events and the confusion 'helped to create the electrically exciting atmosphere that fosters the soul of the nation. The hubbub created during the Eisteddfod week is essential to its success ... I believe that the present pattern is near enough to that which a festival of this kind should be; not a series of "happenings" following each other like a string of onions, but Culture (with a capital C) expressing itself in every dimension.' He believed that the Eisteddfod should expand further, and that there should be provision on the Eisteddfod field for opera and ballet and poetry reading and mime and other cultural activities, together with the usual amenities, so that it would not be necessary for anyone to leave the field even to have a drink.

Despite the tradition of total abstinence among many of the leaders of the Eisteddfod movement, there were others who felt the need for facilities to be installed on the Eisteddfod field which would, in addition to providing beverages for those who require them, prevent the daily drift of young people away from the field to the nearest pub, where some of them were tempted to spend the rest of the day in companionable surroundings, occasionally with boisterous consequences.

The 1974 Eisteddfod returned to a venue which had been the scene of landmarks in its past. The 1451 Eisteddfod at Carmarthen was the first to be known by that name. It was in a garden in Carmarthen, in 1819, that the Gorsedd of Bards of the Isle of Britain held its first assembly in Wales and became an integral part of the Eisteddfod. At the Carmarthen Eisteddfod of 1867, the Crown was first awarded for a long poem in free verse *(pryddest)* and was given equal status to the Chair. The 1911 Eisteddfod, held at Carmarthen, was memorable for the visit of a Welsh choir of seven hundred voices from America.

At the opening ceremony on the Monday morning, a place of honour had been set aside on the Eisteddfod platform for some 300 Welsh language learners, many of whom had pursued their learning at evening classes arranged throughout the previous winter by the local Eisteddfod committee. The president of the day, Lord Chalfont, himself a learner of eighteen months' standing, admitted in his presidential address that he had survived for more than fifty years of an eventful life without knowing more than the words of the Welsh national anthem, but he now realised that the Welshman who does not speak his own tongue was cut off from many of the treasures of artistic and cultural life.

The historic event of 1819 was commemorated at a ceremony held at the Ivy Bush Royal Hotel where Lord Chalfont unveiled a stained glass window by John Petts. The window overlooks the reputed site of the garden in which Iolo Morganwg laid a ring of pebbles in 1819 as the forerunner of the Gorsedd circle.

The failure of youth to fulfil the hope arising from the achievement of a young man at Ruthin was keenly felt when the Crown and the Chair were both awarded to men of riper years. The silver crown, valued at £1,000, was so heavy that a replica of light alloy had to be used to place on the head of W. R. P. George, of Cricieth, for his *pryddest* on the theme *Tân* (Fire), which was based on the story of Prometheus's defiance of Zeus when the father of the gods proposed to destroy mankind because he was disappointed with what he had created. The Chair awarded for an *awdl* to *Y Dewin* (The Magician) was won by Moses Glyn Jones of Mynytho, in the Lleyn peninsula, thus ensuring that the two awards went to Bro Dwyfor, the venue of the 1975 Eisteddfod, which had been proclaimed at Cricieth in June 1974.

The perennial problem of finance became acute with accelerating inflation and the uncertainty of support from the new county and district councils following the reorganization of local government. The Carmarthen Eisteddfod had cost £130,000 to stage and it was feared that the annual cost would shortly be £200,000. In addition, the contract with Messrs Woodhouse for the pavilion, now exceeding £50,000 a year, had come to an end and the Eisteddfod Council had to expedite its plans to provide alternative accommodation. The Council carried out extensive researches and found in favour of a mobile prefabricated structure, made in Germany and used in that country since 1959, which could be built in almost any shape and erected in less than twelve weeks, at an estimated cost of £250,000.

During the Eisteddfod week, the Secretary of State for Wales, the Rt. Hon. John Morris, M.P., made a generous offer of a grant of £50,000 towards the cost of purchase of the new pavilion. The Pavilion Fund now stood at £128,000, most of which had been raised from the profits of successive Eisteddfodau. In view of the uncertainty of the situation the Eisteddfod Council decided to purchase the old Pavilion, along with other buildings and their contents, from Messrs Woodhouse for the sum of £70,000 and these were erected, rather belatedly, at Cricieth in preparation for the 1975 Eisteddfod.

Cricieth was heavily haunted by the memory of Lloyd George. The Eisteddfod field stood within an arrow-shot of his home, Brynawelon, and his place on the platform on the Thursday afternoon was taken by his surviving daughter, Lady Olwen Carey-Evans, who, in her presidential address, revealed how her father used to say that his speeches from the Eisteddfod stage were the most difficult to prepare because he had to avoid any reference to his favourite subject, politics.

The Eisteddfod mourned the death of the scholar and poet Sir Thomas Parry-Williams and decided to perpetuate his memory with a commemorative medal to be awarded annually in recognition of outstanding voluntary effort to promote Welsh culture among young people.

The Welsh 'exiles' at Cricieth included a strong representation from the Argentine, and they were particularly welcomed by the new Archdruid, Bryn (R. Bryn Williams), who had himself been reared in the Welsh settlement in Patagonia. He had been installed Archdruid at the proclamation ceremony held at Cardigan on 28 June 1975 within a circle of stones brought from the Presely Hills, the 'bluestones' which men had venerated and transported to distant Stonehenge nearly five thousand years earlier.

The Eisteddfod was held at Cardigan in 1976 to celebrate the eight-hundredth anniversary of that occasion when 'the Lord Rhys held a special feast at Cardigan castle and arranged two manners of contest, the one between poets and bards, and the other between harpists, *crwth* players, pipers and other musicians, and gave two chairs for the winners'.

The pavilion was erected in a field above the town which, in that rainless summer, soon became arid, and the members of the Gorsedd arriving for the Chairing ceremony in something of a dust storm were light-heartedly compared with 'Bedouin Arabs in search of their camels'.

Proposals for a new purpose-built pavilion, as opposed to the German plans previously adopted, were put forward by the Eisteddfod Council, but these were contested to such an extent that an extraordinary general meeting had to be called later in the year before they could be approved.

The Crown was offered for a poem composed in the style of *penillion telyn* (verses to be sung to the harp) on the theme *Troeon Bywyd* (the twists of Fate), and the identity of its winner was apparent to one of the three adjudicators, at least, and inferred in *Lol*, the magazine of satire and nudity that appeared annually on the Eisteddfod field. This did nothing to diminish the delight of the vast assembly when he stood up and was recognised as the young man who had seized the Crown and the Chair at Ruthin in 1973, Alan Lloyd Roberts (Alan Llwyd), and speculation on the prospect of his ability to repeat that feat, so as to match the achievements of Sir Thomas Parry-Williams at Wrexham (1912) and Bangor (1915) instantly became rife. The literary *cognoscenti* were already satisfied that he would do so, but the ferreters among eisteddfodic secrets prophesied that the contest for the Chair would provide an awkward, yet historic, situation. It was rumoured that the Chair was to be awarded to Dic Jones who had won at Aberafan in 1966 for his memorable awdl to *Y Cynhaeaf* (the Harvest) but this was discounted when it was realised that he was a member of the local literary committee, and, therefore, not eligible to compete. Those who had reasoned in this manner were taken aback when the Archdruid announced that he who had submitted a poem under the pseudonym *Rhos y Gadair,* and who had been awarded the Chair by the adjudicators, had broken the rules of the competition and had, therefore, been disqualified. *Rhos y Gadair,* it soon transpired, was Dic Jones.

By good fortune, there was another outstanding poem among the twenty-five submitted which, the adjudicators had agreed, was also worthy of the Chair. Its author, the Archdruid announced, had not felt able to accept the Chair, in view of the embarrassing situation that had been created but, after lengthy discussion, he had been persuaded to do so. Alan Llwyd was thereupon installed in the Chair and became the second person ever to have won the Chair and the Crown at the same Eisteddfod on two separate occasions.

The eight-hundredth anniversary of that 'special feast' at Cardigan, was universally regarded as a successful and exciting event. The Eisteddfod, despite its age, was young and virile, and perhaps more so than ever.

The Cardigan Eisteddfod forgot to celebrate the hundred-and-fiftieth anniversary of the death of that eccentric and complex troubadour-scholar Iolo Morganwg, who had devised the Gorsedd of Bards and grafted it to the Eisteddfod. He would have been content, however, to see the Professors of Welsh at four of the University Colleges of Wales installed together as honorary members of the Gorsedd, and he would not have minded the admission of a Catholic priest from Dublin, and of the Bishop of Swansea and Brecon, and of the leading Welsh rugby player of the day.

Iolo may chuckle on his cloud to think that he bamboozled our savants for a century and more, but he can also feel a glow of satisfaction for, without his inventive mind, the Eisteddfod could well have become a memory.

THE GORSEDD OF BARDS

Even though the *Gorsedd of Bards of the Isle of Britain* can only be traced to 1792, it has by now acquired a respectable antiquity, and its popular appeal is manifest in the record attendance on the Eisteddfod field on those days when the bardic ceremonies take place. Its contribution to the National Eisteddfod is not only one of colour and pageantry: it plays a leading part in the promotion of Welsh culture and in the fostering of the Welsh language. It has a powerful voice in the deliberations of the National Eisteddfod as more than two-thirds of the members of the Eisteddfod Court are there by virtue of their membership of the Gorsedd.

No National Eisteddfod may be held unless it is proclaimed at least a year and a day in advance by the Gorsedd of Bards. The proclamation takes place within the Gorsedd Circle 'in the face of the sun, the eye of light.'

The circle consists of twelve stone pillars, sometimes hewn from a local quarry, sometimes gathered from the fields, or brought down from the surrounding hills. A large, flat-topped stone, known as the *Maen Llog* (the Logan Stone), lies at the centre of the circle and provides a platform from which the Archdruid conducts the proceedings. Facing it, at the east cardinal point, is *Maen y Cyfamod* (the Stone of the Covenant), at which the Herald Bard stands, and behind this are *Meini'r Porth* (the Portal Stones) which are guarded by purple-robed Eisteddfod officials. The portal stone to the right of the entrance points to sunrise at midsummer day, while that to the left indicates the rising sun at midwinter. The shadows thrown by these three stones form the pattern /|\ symbolising the ineffable name and signifying the rays of the divine attributes — love, justice and truth. This *nod cyfrin* (mystic mark) is known as *Nod Pelydr Goleuni* (the mark of the shafts of light).

The ceremony opens with a flourish of trumpets from the Logan Stone, followed by the Gorsedd prayer:

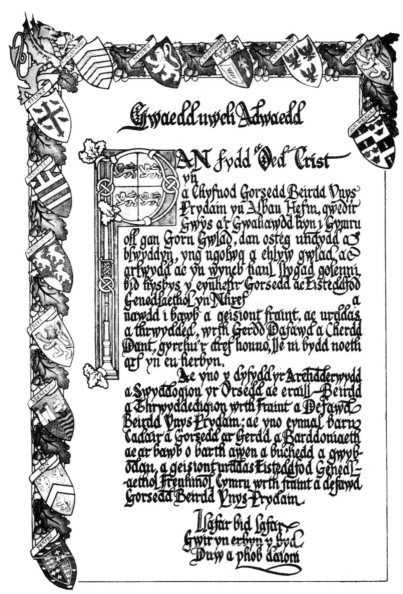

Gwaedd uwch Adwaedd

BLWYDDYN fydd Oed Crist
yn
a Chyfnod Gorsedd Beirdd Ynys
Prydain yn Albau Hefin, gwedi'r
Gwys a'r Gwahawdd hyn i Gymru
oll gan Gorn Gwlad, dan osteg undydd a
blwyddyn, yng ngolwg a chlyw gwlad, ac
arfywdd ac yn wyneb haul llygad goleuni,
bid hysbys y cynhelir Gorsedd ac Eisteddfod
Genedlaethol yn Nhref
a
nawdd i bawb a geisiont fraint, ac urddas,
a thrwydded, wrth Gerdd Dafawd a Cherdd
Dant, gyrchu'r dref honno, lle ni bydd noeth
arf yn eu herbyn.

Ac yno y dyfydd yr Archdderwydd
a Swyddogion yr Orsedd ac eraill Beirdd
a Thrwyddedigion wrth Fraint a Defawd
Beirdd Ynys Prydain; ac yno cynnal barn
Cadair a Gorsedd ar Gerdd a Barddoniaeth
ac ar bawb o barth awen a buchedd a gwyb-
odau, a geisiont urddas Eisteddfod Genedlaethol Frenhinol Cymru wrth fraint a defawd
Gorsedd Beirdd Ynys Prydain.

Llafar bid Llafar
Gwir yn erbyn y byd
Duw a phob daioni

SGRÔL Y CYHOEDDI
(THE PROCLAMATION SCROLL)

137

Grant, O God, Thy protection.
And in protection, strength,
And in strength, understanding,
And in understanding, perception of righteousness,
And in perception of righteousness, the love of it,
And in the love of it, the love of all Life,
And in all Life, to love God,
God and all goodness.

The Archdruid ascends the Logan Stone and performs the opening ceremony by laying his hand on the partially drawn blade of the Grand Sword, calling *A Oes Heddwch?* (Is There Peace?). This he does three times, sheathing the Grand Sword each time the reply *Heddwch!* (Peace!) is echoed by the bards and the people.

The Archdruid then receives *Y Corn Hirlas* (The Hirlas Horn) proffered to him by a local matron. The *Hirlas* was the traditional drinking horn in which the mead or the wine of welcome was offered to the guest: it symbolises the welcome of the neighbourhood to the Eisteddfod. He also receives *Y Flodeuged,* a sheaf of wild flowers, presented by a maiden representing the youth of Wales, who is attended by a group of little girls who dance a floral dance within the circle. The dance is also performed on the Eisteddfod platform following the crowning and chairing ceremonies. Both matron and maiden wear long cloaks of vermilion trimmed with gold, over white silk gowns, and a flowing headdress of gold lamé. The dancers wear short green tunics, with chaplets and garlands of wild flowers. The green, white and blue colours of the bardic gowns, the purple raiment of the Eisteddfod Court officials, the crimson tunics of trumpeters and bannerbearers, the blue mantle of the Herald Bard, the oyster-shell opalescence of the Archdruid's robe, and his regalia of bronze and gold, combine to present a picturesque and colourful ceremony. This is in contrast to the former haphazard and often slipshod nature of the proceedings, which gave rise to considerable criticism and ridicule. The present ritual, elaborated by Cynan, and the discipline introduced by Capt. Geoffrey Crawshay (Sieffre o Gyfarthfa), provides a dignified and impressive ceremony that presents Wales with its one spectacle of colourful pageantry.

No one today claims a druidic ancestry for the Gorsedd, or believes that it is anything more than the creation of a clever and imaginative Welsh stonemason, Iolo Morganwg, who lived in a romantic and neo-druidic age. With his vast knowledge of bardic lore he was able to compose poetry that was accepted as the work of

Dafydd ap Gwilym, and to conceive an extravaganza that was to fool the nation and its scholars for a century and more. Cynan, in his 'I Believe in the Gorsedd of Bards', confides:

> I do not believe in the Druidic ancestry of the Gorsedd, but I do believe in what that imaginative myth symbolises — the rich and splendid tradition of Welsh bardism, which can still be traced as far back as the sixth century.

Cynan also refers to the democratic nature of the Gorsedd: 'in its procession, the University professor may well be walking with a literary village postman or collier and discussing the Englyn of the year'. Those who once jeered and jibed are now proud to receive the honour of bardic rank. Its members come from all walks of life, — peers and prelates, scientists and housewives, trade unionists and members of parliament, roadmen and lords of appeal in ordinary, — drawn together by their common interest in the arts and, in particular, their love for poetry and music. The Queen was admitted an honorary ovate, as Princess Elizabeth, at the Mountain Ash Eisteddfod in 1946, under the bardic title *Elisabeth o Windsor*. Prince Philip *(Philip Meirionnydd)* was invested at Cardiff in 1960. Queen Elizabeth, the Queen Mother *(Betsi o Efrog)*, and the late King George VI, were admitted at Swansea in 1926.

The principal dignitary of the Gorsedd of Bards is the Archdruid. Although Iolo Morganwg assumed the role of presiding druid, 'qualified to initiate worthy poets into the rights and privileges of the Bardic Circle', there is no evidence that he called himself Archdruid, or that this title was used earlier than 1832. At Iolo's death, the leadership passed to his son, Taliesin ab Iolo, who published his father's *Cyfrinach Beirdd Ynys Prydain* and who won the chair at the Cardiff Eisteddfod in 1834 for his ode to *Y Derwyddon* (The Druids). On his death in 1847 there were two aspirants for the supremacy.

The one, Evan Davies (Myfyr Morgannwg: 1801-88), had gained proficiency in the rules of Welsh poetry, and in mathematics, without receiving any formal education. A native of Pencoed, he settled at Pontypridd as a watchmaker. He assumed the bardic name Ieuan Myfyr but later changed it to Myfyr Morgannwg and became an ardent follower of Iolo's druidism and published several books on the subject. After Taliesin's death he conducted druidical rites near Maen Chwyf (the Rocking Stone) at Pontypridd Common, at the equinoxes and solstices, and claimed to be the Archdruid. He

CORON YR ARCHDDERWYDD
Y DEYRNWIALEN A'R DDWYFRONNEG
(THE ARCHDRUID'S CROWN, SCEPTRE AND BREASTPLATE)

appeared on the stage at the Llangollen Eisteddfod in 1858 wearing a 'druidical egg' on a string round his neck!

The other claimant was also sitting on the stage at that Eisteddfod, wearing a white tunic, a scarlet waistcoat, green trousers and, on his head, a huge fox skin hat. He was William Price of Llantrisant (1800-93), physician, surgeon and eccentric. He claimed to be 'the elected successor of the chief druid' and performed druidic rites at Maen Chwyf, over which he wanted to build a tower one hundred feet high, where 'millions, yet unborn, shall assemble to learn the music and the language of our people'. He believed that he would have a son who would succeed him as archdruid and restore the druidic system to its ancient glory. In 1884 he was charged at Cardiff Assizes with attempting to cremate the body of his infant son, Iesu Grist, as a result of which the legality of cremation was established.

The title of Archdruid appears to have been formally used for the first time at the Beaumaris Eisteddfod in 1832, by David James (Dewi o Ddyfed: 1803-71), a native of Manordeifi, who was a curate at Almondbury in Yorkshire and an active member of the Association of Welsh Clergy in the West Riding of the County of York, a society that advocated the appointment of Welsh-speaking bishops and clergy to sees and livings in Wales. He was a prominent figure on the eisteddfod platform and, among other works, he published *The Patriarchal Religion of Britain, or a Complete Manual of Ancient British Druidism*. Although he appears to have acted as Archdruid at Beaumaris there is no evidence that he continued to do so or that he made any effort to retain the title.

The official list of Archdruids begins in 1876 with the installation of Clwydfardd (David Griffiths: 1800-94), a Denbigh clockmaker, at the Wrexham Eisteddfod. Although he claims that he 'was appointed Archdruid in 1860', he agrees that it was at Wrexham that he 'was licensed as Archdruid of the Gorsedd of the Bards of the Isle of Britain'. He had the privilege of investing Queen Marie of Roumania at the Llandudno Eisteddfod in 1890, under the bardic name *Carmen Sylva*, and in 1894, at Caernarfon, he admitted the Prince of Wales and Princess Alexandra.

He was succeeded, after his death in 1894, by Richard Williams (Hwfa Môn: 1823-1895), an Independent minister. Born at Trefdraeth, Anglesey, he moved with his parents at an early age to Rhos-tre-Hwfa near Llangefni. After a period at Fetter Lane Church in London, he returned to Wales in 1881 as minister at Llannerch-y-medd and later at Llangollen. He was admitted a member of the Gorsedd at the Aberffraw Eisteddfod in 1849 and he

GWIALEN YR
ARWYDDFARDD.
(HERALD BARD'S WAND)

Y CLEDDYF MAWR
(GORSEDD GRAND SWORD)

HANNER CLEDD CYD-ORSEDD CYMRU A LLYDAW
(HALF-SWORD, UNITED WITH THE OTHER HALF AT A WALES-BRITTANY
JOINT GORSEDD)

won the Chair at Caernarfon (1862), Mold (1873) and Birkenhead (1878), and the Crown at Carmarthen in 1867. He was elected Archdruid in 1895 and, like his predecessor Clwydfardd, he was an impressive figure on the Logan Stone; his voice, a contemporary reporter attested, 'made the hills echo'.

Evan Rees (Dyfed: 1850-1922) was elected Archdruid in 1896, the year following the death of Hwfa Môn. He was born at Puncheston, in Pembrokeshire, but his parents moved to Aberdare and he found himself working in a colliery when he was eight years of age. He entered the ministry fifteen years later, as a Calvinistic Methodist minister and was later editor of *Y Drysorfa*. He was awarded the Chair at Merthyr Tydfil (1881), Liverpool (1884), Brecon (1889) and Merthyr again in 1901.

In 1923 it was decided that the tenure of the office should be limited to four years. The Archdruid is elected by secret ballot by the Gorsedd Board, consisting of the officers and eighteen elected members, and the appointment is confirmed at the Annual General Meeting of the Gorsedd. He is installed with impressive ritual at the proclamation ceremony following his election.

The first to be installed under the new rule was John Cadvan Davies (Cadfan: 1846-1923), a native of Llangadfan, Montgomeryshire, and a Wesleyan minister. He won the Crown at Liverpool (1884), Caernarfon (1886) and London (1887), and published several volumes of work. He died within a year of his installation.

He was followed, in 1924, by Elfed (the Rev. Elvet Lewis), a native of Cynwyl Elfed near Carmarthen. He won the Chair at Caernarfon (1894) and the Crown at Wrexham (1888) and Brecon (1889), but he will be best remembered for his hymns, some of which are among the finest in the Welsh language. No one will forget the gentle melody in his voice, or his fortitude in his blindness.

Elfed was succeeded, in 1928, by John Owen Williams (Pedrog: 1853-1932), born at Madryn and brought up at Llanbedrog, at the home of relatives after his parents had died while he was still a child. He started work as a gardener at twelve years of age and, in 1884, became minister of Kensington Congregational Church, Liverpool, where he remained until his retirement in 1930. He won the Chair at Swansea (1891), Llanelli (1895) and Liverpool (1900) and he was awarded the gold medal at the Utica Eisteddfod in 1889.

Dr J. Gwili Jenkins (Gwili: 1872-1936) was appointed Archdruid in succession to Pedrog and he officiated at the Aberafan Eisteddfod in 1932. A native of Hendy, near Pontarddulais, he began his education at Gwynfryn, Watcyn Wyn's school at Ammanford, and went to Bangor, Cardiff and Jesus College, Oxford, following which he succeeded Watcyn Wyn at Gwynfryn. He eventually became professor of New Testament Exegesis at the Baptist College, Bangor, and at the University College there. He was a man of considerable learning and the fruits of his research appeared in his *Hanfod Duw a Pherson Crist*. As Archdruid he was conscious of the need for reform and for closer collaboration between the Gorsedd and the National Eisteddfod Council.

Gwili was succeeded by J. J. Williams (J.J.), Congregational minister at Morriston, who had won the Chair at Caernarfon (1906) for his *awdl* to *Y Lloer* and at Llangollen in 1908. He was installed at the Fishguard Eisteddfod, on 4th August 1936, by the deputy-archdruid, Elfed. In that year, it was decided that the Archdruid's term of office should be limited to three years but, owing to the war, this was not implemented.

Crwys (W. Crwys Williams) was installed Archdruid on the eve of the Second World War, in 1939, and he retained the office for the duration of the war. Crwys had been awarded the Crown at Colwyn Bay (1910), Carmarthen (1911) and Corwen (1919) and the lyrical quality of his shorter poems caused him to be one of the most popular Welsh poets of his time. He was a Congregational minister, and he was widely known throughout Wales as Secretary of the British and Foreign Bible Society, and also as a humorist and wit.

Wil Ifan (the Rev. William Evans) was installed in succession to Crwys at the proclamation of the Colwyn Bay Eisteddfod in 1947. He had won the Crown at Abergavenny (1913), Birkenhead (1917) and Pwllheli (1925).

At the proclamation ceremony of the Llanrwst Eisteddfod, in June 1950, Cynan, who had been Recorder of the Gorsedd since 1935, became Archdruid. Cynan (Albert Evans Jones, later Sir Cynan Evans Jones), a native of Pwllheli, was ordained during active service in Macedonia and returned to officiate with the Methodists at Penmaenmawr. He then served as an extra-mural lecturer under the University College of Wales, Bangor, and achieved distinction as a lecturer and as a drama producer. It was his feeling for pageantry and his dramatic expertise that enabled him to bring dignity to the ceremonial of the Gorsedd. He won the Crown at Caernarfon (1921), Mold (1923) and Bangor (1931), and the Chair at Pontypool in 1924 for his outstanding ode *I'r Duw Nid Adwaenir* (To the Unknown God).

Dyfnallt Owen (Dyfnallt) was born at Llangiwc, in Glamorgan, and began life in the coalmines at the age of twelve. He later became a Congregational minister. He was over eighty years of age when he was installed Archdruid at Ystradgynlais in 1954, after being a member of the Gorsedd for sixty years. He won the Crown at the Swansea Eisteddfod in 1907.

William Morris, a native of Ffestiniog, and Presbyterian minister at Caernarfon, succeeded Dyfnallt in 1957. He was a close friend and benefactor of Hedd Wyn, the poet of the Black Chair of Birkenhead. He was awarded the Chair at the Neath Eisteddfod in 1934.

Trefin (Edgar Phillips) was installed Archdruid in succession to William Morris at the proclamation ceremony held within the walls of Cardiff Castle in 1959. Born at Trefin, in Pembrokeshire, he began life as a tailor and entered the scholastic profession after service in the 1914-18 war. He became a member of the Gorsedd in 1924 and, in 1947, he was appointed Grand Sword-bearer: he used to say that it was his training, carrying 200 pounders in the First War, that enabled him to bear the Grand Sword with such apparent ease. He won the Chair at the Wrexham Eis .dfod in 1933.

Cynan, in succeeding Trefin in 1963, became the first person ever to be elected Archdruid for the second time, as he was also to become the first Archdruid to be President of the National Eisteddfod on his election to that office in 1967.

Gwyndaf succeeded Cynan as Archdruid in 1966, and also succeeded him as Recorder in 1970. A native of Llanfachreth, in Meirioneth, he gained early distinction as a *penillion* singer and as a poet. In 1933 he won the Inter-college Eisteddfod chair for his ode to *Deirdre'r Gofidiau* (Deirdre of the Sorrows), which was the first *awdl* to be composed in *verse libre*. He was awarded the Chair at the Caernarfon Eisteddfod in 1934 for his *Magdalen,* in which he also experimented with *cynghanedd* in free verse.

Tilsli (Gwilym Tilsley) was installed Archdruid in succession to Gwyndaf at the proclamation of the Ammanford Eisteddfod. A native of Llanidloes, he graduated at Aberystwyth and at Cambridge before becoming a Wesleyan minister. He was awarded the Chair at Caerffili in 1950 for his *Awdl Foliant i'r Glowr* (Ode in Praise of the Collier) and at Llangefni in 1957 for his *Cwm Carnedd.*

Brinli (Brinley Richards) was the first lawyer to be appointed Archdruid: he had been one of the honorary legal advisers to the Eisteddfod since 1957. He was born at Nant-y-ffyllon and was active in local government at Maesteg for over forty years. He won several prizes for satirical poems at the National Eisteddfod before

GORSEDD BEIRDD YNYS PRYDAIN

HYN SYDD I ARWYDDO
BOD
WEDI LLWYDDO YN
ARHOLIAD YR ORSEDD
A'I DDERBYN I URDD
Y BARDD YN
EISTEDDFOD GENEDLAETHOL
19
I'W ADNABOD YNG NGHORSEDD
FEL

ARCHDDERWYDD

COFIADUR

Y GWIR YN ERBYN Y BYD

TYSTYSGRIF YR ORSEDD

he was awarded the Chair at Llanrwst in 1951 for his *awdl* to *Y Dyffryn* (The Valley).

Bryn (Bryn Williams), who succeeded Brinli at the proclamation ceremony at Cardigan in 1975, was taken from his native Blaenau Ffestiniog to Patagonia at an early age. When he returned to Wales, at the age of twenty-one, he had to learn English in order to pursue an academic career, for he had been brought up to speak Welsh and Spanish. He won the Chair at Swansea in 1964 for his *awdl* to *Patagonia,* and at Barry in 1968, for his poem to *Y Morwr* (The Sailor) which he had written during a voyage to Patagonia.

Archdruids are appointed from the ranks of *prifeirdd*, those who have won the Chair or the Crown at the National Eisteddfod, but, from time to time, representations were made that the office should be open to those whose achievements were other than in the poetic arts. One of the leading protagonists in this matter was Canon Maurice Jones (Meurig Prysor), Principal of St. David's College, Lampeter, and Gorsedd Treasurer from 1925 to 1938. In 1935 he was very nearly successful in his candidature, despite the limiting regulations, and, in the following year, he was appointed *Bardd yr Orsedd*, an appointment hitherto held by a leading *prifardd*. He nevertheless persisted in his efforts to remove the restriction on election to the highest office and, in 1947, he was appointed *Derwydd Gweinyddol* (the Attendant Druid), a position specially created to honour a person of distinction who was not a *prifardd* and therefore not eligible to be Archdruid. This appointment has been held since that date by the following:

Caerwyn (Owen Ellis Roberts)	1955-1959
Dr Morgan Watcyn	1959-1964
T. H. Lewis (Tybiefab)	1964-1966
Dr Emyr Wyn-Jones (Emyr Wyn Feddyg)	1967-

The earliest Recorder of whom we have knowledge was Eifionydd (John Thomas: 1848-1922) who held office from 1876 until his death. He was succeeded by the journalist and dramatist Beriah Gwynfe Evans (1848-1927), who was followed by his son-in-law, Gwilym Rhug. In 1931, Gwylfa (Rev. Gwylfa Roberts), who had won the Crown at Blaenau Ffestiniog in 1898 and at Cardiff in 1899, was appointed Recorder but he again only held the appointment for a short term.

The office acquired a new dimension with the appointment of Cynan in 1935. In collaboration with Capt. Geoffrey Crawshay, the Herald Bard, he introduced a discipline among the bards and gave form to their ritual. His tenure, extending over a period of 35 years, will remain a unique contribution in the history of the National Eisteddfod.

While Cynan was Archdruid in 1950-54, his place as Recorder was taken by Erfyl Fychan, the Herald Bard, and in 1963-66 by T. W. Thomas (Ab Eos), the Eisteddfod Treasurer.

In 1970, following Cynan's death, Gwyndaf was appointed Recorder.

The first Herald Bard recorded by that name was the Cardiff artist and naturalist Thos. Henry Thomas (Arlunydd Pen-y-garn: 1839-1915) who was appointed in 1895.

Capt. Geoffrey Crawshay (Sieffre o Gyfarthfa) was Herald Bard from 1926 to 1947.

Capt. R. W. Jones (Erfyl Fychan) held the office from 1947 to 1967.

He was succeeded by the author.

CYNGHANEDD

'Beth yw cynghanedd?' — 'What is cynghanedd?' asked some-one four hundred years ago, and got the answer: 'Cydateb cyt-soniaid a chyfnewid bogaliaid' (The correspondence of conso-nants and interchange of vowels). *Geiriadur Prifysgol Cymru* (The University of Wales Dictionary) defines it as 'a system of con-sonance or alliteration in a line of Welsh poetry in strict metre and internal rhyming,' while Professor Gwyn Williams, in *An Introduction to Welsh Poetry*, states that 'the word *cynghanedd* means harmony, and in poetry it is a means of giving pattern to a line by the echoing of sounds, consonantal and vowel.' This pattern is governed by strict rules, not only of consonance and rhyme, but also of accent.

The great master of Welsh prosody, Sir John Morris-Jones, reminds us that 'poetry sprang from song, song itself from singing-together, and singing-together from the flood of feeling in the primitive dance . . . In short, song and tune and dance were all one . . . and one feature was common to them, namely a regular move-ment, or rhythm . . . rhythm made, and makes, poetry what it is.'

Much use is made in early Welsh poetry of repeated sounds in order to emphasize the rhythm, and to indicate the end of a move-ment or line. The repetition of consonants produces consonance; the echoing of syllables yields rhyme. From the special emphasis placed on the matching of consonants in a line of poetry emerged *cynghanedd*.

The poems of Aneirin and Taliesin, dating from the sixth century but available to us from a thirteenth century manuscript, have traces of corresponding consonants, and so have the verses found written in the margin of the Juvencus metrical version of the Psalms, the oldest Welsh poetry extant in manuscript, written in the early part of the ninth century. But it was the *Gogynfeirdd*, the class of bards that flourished from the beginning of the twelfth century to the middle of the fourteenth, who developed its use and insisted that each line should have, in the words of a fifteenth century poet:

> Mesur glân a chynghanedd
> A synnwyr wiw, sain aur wedd

(A clean metre and cynghanedd, and proper sense and sublime sound like gold).

The cynganeddion are divided into four main classes, with subdivisions or refinements:

(a) *Cynghanedd Groes* (cross cynghanedd), in which the consonants in the first half of a line are repeated in the same order in the second half, except at the end of each half, where they must differ:

> Dolau glas | a deiliog lwyn.
> **d l gl (s) | d l g l (n)**

(Green meadows and a leafy tree).

As the end of each half of the line may be either accented or unaccented, there are four sub-divisions of *Cynghanedd Groes*, although the fourth is hardly every used:

> (i) Y llwybrau gynt | lle bu'r gân.
>   **ll   br   g | ll   b   r g´**

(The paths that once knew song)

> (ii) Teg edrych | tuag adref.
>   **t g´dr ˇ | t g´dr ˇ**

(It is fine to face homeward)

> (iii) Afal Awst | o felyster.
>   **f l   st | f l´st ˇ**

(An August apple of sweetness)

> (iv) Fwyn a diwair | f'enaid yw.
>   **f n d wˇ | f n d w**

(Gentle and pure, my soul is she)

The balanced forms, (i) and (ii), are known as *Cynghanedd Groes Rywiog* and in these the two parts of the line may be interchanged:

> (i) Yr ydwyf i | ar dy fedd.
>   Ar dy fedd | yr ydwyf i.
>   **r d f | r d f**

(I am upon thy grave)

(ii) Wedi trawster | daw tristwch
Daw tristwch | wedi trawster
d   tr′st   ˇ | d   tr   ′ st ˇ

(After violence comes sorrow)

In *Cynghanedd Groes o Gyswllt* the last consonant or two of the first part of the line are 'borrowed' by the second part:

(i) Dymor hud | a miri haf
d m r h′(d | m r h′

(Season of magic and summer merriment)

(ii) A bwrlwm aber | i lamu heibio
b rl m′(bˇr | l m   ′ bˇ

(iii) Be caid neb | i'w cydnabod
b c d n′(b)| c dn′ b ˇ

(If someone could be found to acknowledge them)

(b) *Cynghanedd Draws* has a correspondence of consonants at the beginning and at the end of a line, but there is a gap in the middle in which the consonants are not matched. As in *Cynghanedd Groes*, there are sub-divisions based on accent and the balance:

(i) Twrw'r dŵr | man lle torrai'r don
t   r   r d′ |(m n ll) t rr   r d′

(The tumult of water where the wave breaks)

(ii) Ag oerwynt | hydre'n gyrru
g   ′r   ˇ | (dr n)g′ rr ˇ

(With the cold wind of autumn driving)

(iii) Mae'r haf | wedi marw hefyd
m   r h′f | (d) m r   h′f ˇ

(The summer has died also)

(c) *Cynghanedd Sain* has internal rhyme and matching consonants. The line is divided into three parts, the first and second of which rhyme, and consonants in the second part are repeated in the third. It has four classifications based on the accented or unaccented nature of the second and third parts of the line:

(i) Segurdod | yw clod | y cledd
| cl⌐ | cl′

(Idleness is the glory of the sword)

(ii)   Mae'r ad<u>ar</u> | cynn<u>ar</u> | yn canu
          | c′nn ˘ | c′n ˘

(The early birds are singing)

(iii)   Pob gl<u>ân</u> | i l<u>ân</u> | a luniwyd
          | l′n | l′n ˘

(Each fair one for a fair one is fashioned)

(iv)   Llyg<u>aid</u> | a ddyw<u>aid</u> | i ddoeth
          | dd′ ˘ | dd ′

(Eyes speak to the wise)

In *Sain o Gyswllt* the last consonant in one part of a line may be 'borrowed' by the next part:

Oni'th gaf | araf | forwyn
    (f | r ˘ |f′r ˘

(Unless I have you gentle maiden)

Arglwyddes | a santes | oedd
      | s′ ˘(s | ′

(A peeress and a saint she was)

(d) *Cynghanedd Lusg* is the simplest form of *cynghanedd*. It has none of the consonantal echoings of the other forms and consists of an internal rhyme whereby the last syllable of the first half of the line rhymes with the penultimate syllable.

Pan dd<u>êl</u> | yr haf hirf<u>e</u>lyn

(When the long yellow summer comes)

Yng ngwl<u>ad</u> | y pomgran<u>ad</u>au

(In the land of the pomegranates)

The rhyme is sometimes hidden by linking with the next word:

Paun asgell-l<u>as d</u>)inas<u>d</u>ai

(The blue winged peacock of the city houses)

Cynghanedd, like music, is for the ear and it is therefore permitted to match corresponding sounds, such as *ff* and *ph*, *r* and *rh*.

A <u>ph</u>lwm a dur | yn <u>ff</u>lam dân

(And lead and steel a fiery flame)

Eithr angau | a aeth rhyngom
(But death did come between us)

The soft consonants *b, d, g* harden when repeated:

Y ddraig goch | ddyry cychwyn
  ddr g g ch | dd r c′ ch ˘
(The red dragon leads the way)

or when followed by *h:*

Gair teg | a wna gariad hir
  g r t′ | g r d h′
(A soft word makes for long lasting love)

Double consonants (only *n* and *r* may be doubled in Welsh) count as one:

Co<u>n</u>wy | mewn dyffryn cy<u>nn</u>es
(Conway in a warm valley)

Although it is necessary in *Cynghanedd Groes* for there to be a complete matching of consonants in both parts of the line, it is permissible for *n* to stand unmatched at the beginning of the first half:

Yn dawnsio'r nos | dan sêr nen
 (n)d ns   r n′ | d n s r n′
(Dancing the night under the stars of heaven)

And when *n* appears alone at the beginning of the second part it is tolerated and the *cynghanedd* is classified as *Croes* rather than *Draws:*

Y gawod ddail | yn gad ddu
  g   d dd′ | (n)g d dd′
(The shower of leaves a black host)

Apart from such concessions, the discipline of *cynghanedd* is unrelenting.

Efforts to repeat its magic in English verse have failed, though the Dorset poet, William Barnes, made a bold attempt with such lines as:

Do lean down low in Linden Lea.

Other English poets made similar attempts, including Dylan Thomas and Gerard Manley Hopkins, who prettily described *cynghanedd* as 'a consonantal chiming'. None, however, was able to make it his handmaiden, and it remains as something quite unique to the Welsh language.

THE TWENTY-FOUR METRES

The art and techniques of Welsh poetry were handed down by word of mouth from earliest times and it is not until the fourteenth century that we have evidence of any instruction being committed to writing. The oldest extant work is *Cerddwriaeth Cerdd Dafawd,* a bardic grammar which is believed to have been compiled by Einion Offeiriad, a poet-priest, 'in honour and in praise of Sir Rhys ap Gruffydd' to whom he had also composed a panegyric ode in about 1320. It was probably edited and enlarged by Dafydd Ddu Athro o Hiraddug before the end of the century, and the earliest version of the work appears in *Llyfr Coch Hergest* (the Red Book of Hergest) in about 1400. It contains the basic elements of Welsh grammar, together with an abridgement of the Latin grammar that was used in schools in the Middle Ages, and describes *Pedwar Mesur ar hugain Cerdd Dafod* (twenty-four metres of poetic art).

Gutun Owain, a noted transcriber of manuscripts, compiled his own grammar in 1455 under the title *Cyfrinach Beirdd Ynys Prydain* (The Secret of the Bards of the Isle of Britain), a title which was later purloined by Iolo Morganwg. There followed *Pum Llyfr Cerddwriaeth* (The Five Books of Minstrels) by Simwnt Fychan in 1575 and grammars by Sion Dafydd Rhys in 1592 and Captain William Middleton in 1593.

The rules of Welsh prosody were obviously discussed at early eisteddfodau. At the Carmarthen Eisteddfod *c.* 1451, Dafydd ab Edmwnd was awarded the chair, not for the best *awdl* but for his rearrangement of the twenty-four metres. The growing nuisance of roving rhymers and pretentious poetasters had made it necessary to impose a discipline and this was achieved by making it more difficult for poets to qualify for the rank of *pencerdd.* A poet wishing to obtain this rank was expected to compose an *awdl* which contained each of the twenty-four metres and it was considered that the most effective way of maintaining the standards of poetic art was to make the metres more difficult. Dafydd ab Edmwnd succeeded in this respect and, furthermore, he invented two new metres in which neither he nor any other poet was ever able to compose anything sensible let alone poetical: they were simply meant as a form of examination exercise and could serve no other purpose. It is small wonder, therefore, that there was considerable opposition to Dafydd ab Edmwnd's codification, especially from the poets of South Wales.

Dafydd's arrangement was officially adopted at the Caerwys Eisteddfod in 1523 through the influence of his nephew, Tudur Aled, who was the chaired bard at that Eisteddfod and, from that time forth, his classification was the one used in illustrative odes. By the eighteenth century it had become customary to compose *awdlau* containing examples of all the metres, even among poets of the calibre of Goronwy Owen who wrote three such odes, including his *Marwnad Lewis Morris* (Elegy to Lewis Morris).

The twenty-four metres are divided into three groups, dealing with *englyn*, *cywydd* and *awdl* measures. They may be summarised as follows:

I   Englyn Measures

1.   *Englyn penfyr* consists of 16 syllables divided into two lines, of 10 and 6 syllables, that is a *toddaid byr* (see 19), to which is added a line of 7 syllables, hence *penfyr* (brief ending). It is the measure used in the verses attributed to Heledd lamenting the death of her brothers in battle against the English and the desolation that followed the burning of the hall of Cynddylan, her favourite brother, at Pengwern (Shrewsbury).

> Stafell Cynddylan ys tywyll heno
> heb dan heb wely
> wylaf wers tawaf wedy.

(Cynddylan's hall, it is dark tonight: no fire, no bed. I shall weep awhile and then I shall be silent).

2.   *Englyn milwr* (soldier's englyn) has three rhyming lines of 7 syllables, which was said to be 'the manner in which the soldiers sang of old.' Llywarch Hen, a prince in Powys in the sixth century, having seen his twenty-four sons killed fighting the Mercians, bemoans his fate:

Baglan bren neud cynhaeaf
rhudd rhedyn melyn calaf
neur digerais a garaf.

(O my wooden crutch, it is harvest-time; the bracken is red, the
stubble yellow. Whom I once despised I now love).

3. *Englyn unodl union* combines a *toddaid byr* (19) with a
cywydd deuair hirion (10) and thus consists of four lines of 10,
6, 7 and 7 syllables respectively, all rhyming. This is the most
frequently used form of *englyn* and is by far the best known,
but its intricacies make it one of the most difficult poetic forms
to compose in world literature. The following example was
written by Ieuan Brydydd Hir on seeing the ruins of the court
of Ifor Hael, lord of Bassaleg and patron of Dafydd ap
Gwilym:

Llys Ifor Hael, gwael yw'r gwedd, — yn garnau
  Mewn gwerni mae'n gorwedd,
  Drain ac ysgall mall a'i medd,
  Mieri lle bu mawredd.

(The court of Ifor Hael, sad is its appearance: it lies in heaps
among alder trees: a profusion of thorns and thistles possess it:
briars where greatness lay).

4. *Englyn unodl crwca* is an *englyn unodl union* in reverse,
in that the couplet comes first, followed by the *toddaid byr*.

  Mae y gŵr yn ymguraw,
  A'i dylwyth yn wyth neu naw,
Dan oer hin yn dwyn y rhaw — mewn trymwaith
  Bu ganwaith heb giniaw.

(The man is assiduous; he must provide for a family of eight or
nine. In cold weather he bears his spade in heavy toil. A
hundred times has he gone without his dinner).

5. *Englyn cyrch* consists of two couplets, one of a *cywydd
deuair hirion* (10) and the other of an *awdl-gywydd* (9).

6. *Englyn proest dalgron* comprises four lines of 7 syllables,
each ending in *proest*, a kind of half-rhyme in which the final
consonants correspond.

7. *Englyn lleddfbroest* is the same except that the lines must

end in dipthong, with or without a consonant following the dipthong.

8.   *Englyn proest gadwynog* has four half-rhyming lines but each alternate line rhymes fully.

II   Cywydd Measures
9.   *Awdl-gywydd* consists of couplets of seven-syllable lines. The last syllable in the first line in each couplet rhymes with the caesura in the second line, the last syllable of which provides the main rhyme:

> Llawenaf lle o Wynedd
> Yw llys medd a llysiau Môn

(The happiest place in Gwynedd is the court of Anglesey where mead and herbs are served).

10.   *Cywydd deuair hirion* has rhyming couplets of 7 syllables, with the rhyme accented and unaccented alternately. It has been the commonest measure in use in the strict metre since it was popularised by Dafydd ap Gwilym in the fourteenth century. The following invitation to a nun to abandon her convent for the freedom of the woods is attributed to him, though it is more probably the work of an unknown poet of the fifteenth century:

> Paid, er Mair, â'r pader main,
> A chrefydd myneich Rhufain . . .
> Dy grefydd, deg oreuferch,
> Y sydd wrthwyneb i serch . . .
> Dyred i'r fedw gadeiriog
> I grefydd y gwŷdd a'r gog.

(Give up, by Mary, the rosary of precious stones, and the religion of the monks of Rome . . . Thy religion, fairest of maidens, is the antithesis of love . . . Come to the spreading birch tree, to the religion of the trees and the cuckoo).

11.   *Cywydd deuair fyrion* comprises rhyming couplets of 4 syllables which, on account of its limitations, is rarely used:

> It, ferch, serch sydd,
> Lawn lawenydd;
> Da wyt a doeth,
> Eurddawn, wirddoeth.

(Thou, sweet maiden, hast charm, full of joy; virtuous thou
art, golden-gifted, truly wise).

12. *Cywydd llosgyrnog* was borrowed from a Latin hymn
form and comprises two (sometimes three or four) rhyming
lines of 8 syllables, followed by a *llosgwrn* (tail) of 7 syllables
which internally rhymes with the couplet but also carries the
main rhyme:

> Y mae goroff em a garaf
> O gof aelaw ag a folaf
>> O choeliaf gael ei chalon,
> Am na welais i, myn Elien,
> O Lanurful i lyn Aerfen
>> Wawr mor wen o'r morynion

(There is a splendid gem I love, of sweet remembrance, whom
I worship, I trust I shall win her heart. For I have not seen, by
Elien, from Llanurful to Aerfen lake, one so fair among the
maidens).

III Awdl Measures

13. *Rhupunt* is a primitive measure in which a line is
divided into three parts of 4 syllables each, the first two parts
rhyming, and the third carrying the main rhyme:

> Och o'r colled | am eil Luned | em oleuni!
> Och o'r trymfyd | a llwyr dristyd | fod llawr drosti!

(O the loss of the peerless Luned, gem of light! O the sadness
and utter sorrow that the turf should lie upon her).

14. *Cyhydedd fer* is a rhyming couplet of eight-syllable lines,
usually a sequence of couplets using the same rhyme. It was
used by Taliesin in the sixth century:

> Arwŷre gwyr Catraeth gan ddydd
> am wledig gweithfuddig gwarthegydd ...
> Ni roddes na maes na choedydd
> achles i ormes pan ddyfydd

(The men of Catraeth rise at dawn for a triumphant, cattle-
providing prince ... Nor field nor forest provided a refuge for
tyranny when it came).

15. *Byr a thoddaid* is a combination of *cyhydedd fer* (14) and *toddaid byr* (19).

16. *Clogyrnach* is made up of a couplet of *cyhydedd fer* (14) followed by a measure similar to *toddaid byr* (19) but of a different rhyming pattern.

17. *Cyhydedd naw ban* has lines of 9 syllables arranged in a series of couplets all with the same rhyme.

18. *Cyhydedd hir* is a line of 19 syllables usually divided into sections of 5,5,5 and 4 syllables, the first three rhyming and the last carrying the main rhyme.

19. *Toddaid* has 19 syllables, divided into lines of 10 and 9 syllables, with the main rhyme occuring at the seventh, eighth or ninth syllable of the first line and the end of the first rhyming with the middle of the second line:

> Ban aeth gwroliaeth ar elawr — o'r llys,
> Bu bobl 'i ynys heb eu blaenawr

(When courage departed on a bier from the court the people of his island were without their leader).

A 16 syllable version of this measure, divided into lines of 10 and 6 syllables, is known as *Toddaid byr,* and is familiar as it forms the first two lines of *englyn unodl union* (3):

> Y llynnau gwyrddion llonydd — a gysgant
> Mewn gwasgod o fynydd.

(The still, green lakes that sleep in a shady place in the mountain).

20. *Gwawodyn* consists of a couplet of nine-syllable lines followed by a *toddaid:*

> Aur glân ag arian yma gerir,
> Ag o wan allu a gynullir;
> A da'r byd i gyd a gedwir — dros bryd,
> A da'r byd i gyd yma gedir.

(Pure gold and silver are here treasured, and in our weakness we hoard them; the world's goods we keep awhile, the world's goods are all left here).

21. *Gwawdodyn hir* is the same, except that more than one couplet precedes the *toddaid*.

22. *Hir a thoddaid* is similar to the *gwawdodyn hir* except that the lines are of ten syllables. It is a popular measure which frequently features in *awdlau,* for example in Dic Jones's chair-winning poem to *Y Cynhaeaf* (The Harvest).

> Doed y dwyreinwynt a'r gyrwynt garwaf,
> I mi rhag newyn mae aur gynhaeaf,
> Doed eira, cesair, doed y rhew casaf,
> I'r fuches gynnes bydd gwlithog wanaf
> O luniaeth helaeth yr haf — a diddos
> Wâl ym min nos tan y C'lamai nesaf.

(Come the east wind and the wild hurricane, to keep me from hunger there is a golden harvest. Come snow and hail, come the fiercest frost, for the warm herd there will be a dewy swath of the abundant sustenance of summer and a snug bed each evening until next May day).

23. *Cyrch-a-chwta* comprises six lines of seven syllables followed by an *awdl-gywydd*(9)

24. *Tawddgyrch cadwynog* consists of two stanzas of *Rhupunt* (13) except that the rhyming is modified.

The last three measures are said to have been devised by Einion Offeiriad, or by Dafydd Ddu Athro.

INDEX